HOMESPUN FUN

More Than 250 Kid-Tested Activities,
Games, Projects, and Party Ideas
Compiled from the Best Suggestions
of Parents, Grandparents,
Educators, and Children

the mother connection Inc.

St. Martin's Griffin
New York

Library of Congress Cataloging-in-Publication Data

Homespun fun : more than 250 kid-tested
    activities, games, projects, and party
    ideas compiled from the best suggestions
    of parents, grandparents, educators, and
    children / by the Mother Connection.
        p.   cm.
    ISBN 0-312-14617-5
    1. Amusements.   2. Games.   3. Creative
activities and seat work.   I. Mother
Connection (Organization)
GV1203.H568   1996
790.1'922—dc20   96-25605
                                  CIP

First published in The United States of
America by The Mother Connection

First St. Martin's Griffin Edition: November 1996

10 9 8 7 6 5 4 3 2 1

WARNING: All play activities described in this book should be conducted under adult supervision. Some activities require more physical ability or judgment than others and may be dangerous for younger children. Therefore, parents or guardians must exercise care that activities selected are appropriate for the age and abilities of the children participating. You use this book at your own risk, since neither The Mother Connection, Inc., its members, nor the publishers of or any contributor to this book shall have any liability whatsoever for any injury, loss, or damage of any kind to any person resulting directly or indirectly from use of this book.

The Mother Connection, Inc. (TMC) is a non-profit organization based in Andover, Massachusetts, which provides social, educational, and recreational activities and information to families with young children. Founded in 1982, TMC offers a Family Resource Center, a Resource Office, a Toy and Babysitting Cooperative, a Play Space, and a Library. TMC also offers workshops, field trips, special events, and speakers.

The TMC newsletter, published nine times a year, brings together the information and resources of TMC to over 500 families in 45 communities. Over one hundred volunteers of TMC work and play together to ensure that TMC is available to provide friendship and support to all, especially those parents who are new to parenthood or to the region.

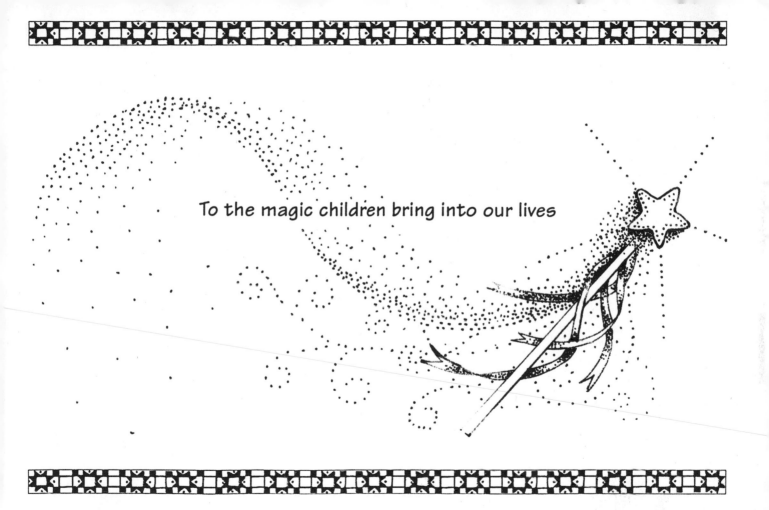

To the magic children bring into our lives

ACKNOWLEDGMENTS

There are many people we would like to thank for making this book possible. First and foremost, we would like to thank all of the people, young and old, who contributed to this book. Their stories enrich this book and make it unique with a tapestry of family histories.

Special thanks to our husbands for putting up with us while we spent every spare moment writing, editing, illustrating and fundraising for this book, and to our children who happily tried out the many wonderful ideas submitted to us.

We would also like to thank the four boards of The Mother Connection, Inc. who were involved in this project.

President Norma Villarreal and her board (1990-91) gave us the green light to begin this book. President Susan Richardson and her boards (1991-93) gave us tremendous support and encouragement throughout this project. And finally, President Sumi Dolben and her board (1993-94) saw this book through to completion.

Many thanks to Hunneman & Company and Victor Company Inc. who offered us the use of their facilities for our two phonathons to solicit activities.

Finally, we are indebted to the following businesses and individuals whose generous sponsorship allowed us to create this beautiful book:

DONORS

John Cusack
Realtor

Leona DeMartino
Century 21, Minuteman Realty

Christine Estabrook
Silverado Athletic Club

William & Barbara Maren
Victor Real Estate

FRIENDS

Daher's For Kids, Andover

Coletta Fanuele
RE/MAX Preferred, Inc.

Elke Kappeler
RE/MAX Preferred, Inc.

Chip Will
Learning Express, Andover

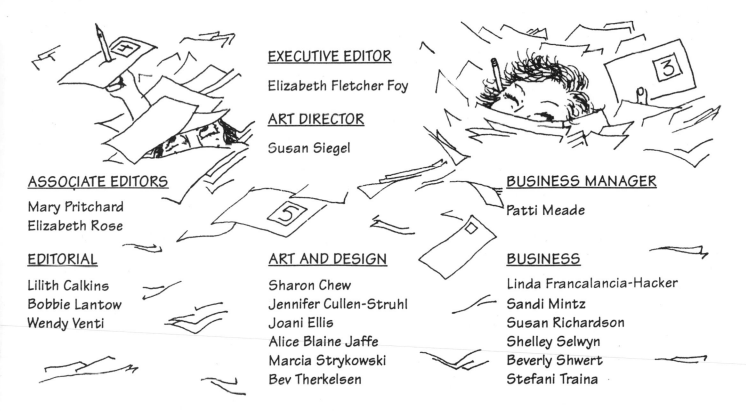

EXECUTIVE EDITOR

Elizabeth Fletcher Foy

ART DIRECTOR

Susan Siegel

ASSOCIATE EDITORS

Mary Pritchard
Elizabeth Rose

BUSINESS MANAGER

Patti Meade

EDITORIAL

Lilith Calkins
Bobbie Lantow
Wendy Venti

ART AND DESIGN

Sharon Chew
Jennifer Cullen-Struhl
Joani Ellis
Alice Blaine Jaffe
Marcia Strykowski
Bev Therkelsen

BUSINESS

Linda Francalancia-Hacker
Sandi Mintz
Susan Richardson
Shelley Selwyn
Beverly Shwert
Stefani Traina

CONTENTS

"What do you and your children enjoy doing together?" This was a question we asked many people--both friends and members of The Mother Connection--as we gathered ideas for this book. Our goal was to capture in writing some of the special times parents have shared with their children. The result is HOMESPUN FUN, a rich collection of magical moments, happy memories, and just plain fun activities to do with your children.

The ideas of over 180 parents, grandparents, educators, and children have been woven together to create HOMESPUN FUN. Like a handstitched quilt that is lovingly passed down from one generation to the next, many of the ideas in this book have been fondly remembered from the contributors' own childhoods.

As we compiled HOMESPUN FUN, we were struck time and again by the ingenuity and simplicity of most of the activities. We felt that this was surely the wisdom of the book, teaching us that magical moments are always there, whether we are taking a walk in the woods, cooped up inside on a rainy day, or putting our children to bed.

There are over 250 activities in HOMESPUN FUN. As you read this book, you will find that some of the activities are attributed to more than one person. When we received similar ideas, we merged them into one activity and gave each author credit.

Although HOMESPUN FUN is intended for children from birth to age eight, many of its activities are easily adaptable to older children.

At the end of each of HOMESPUN FUN's nine chapters is a section of helpful hints, chock-full of creative parenting ideas. In addition, we have included an alphabetical index to help you find activities that appeal to you and your children.

HOMESPUN FUN was conceived as an opportunity for people to share ideas and experiences that have made a difference with their families. Throughout this project, the members of our committee have felt an overwhelming enthusiasm for this book. The Mother Connection is a volunteer organization that devotes itself to supporting families. We see in HOMESPUN FUN the spirit of The Mother Connection.

One of the greatest joys and challenges of parenthood is to look for and take advantage of life's magical moments. In reading and using HOMESPUN FUN, we hope you are inspired to share the magic of childhood with your children.

LET'S PRETEND COSTUMES AND GAMES

DRESS-UP TRUNK

A thrift shop is a wonderful place to collect an inexpensive treasure trove of dress-up clothes. Accessories are equally important, so be sure to stock your dress-up trunk with jewelry, wigs, hats, shoes, scarves, and ties. Visit shops after major holidays to purchase props, such as helmets, swords, and magic wands at sale prices. Collect some open-ended materials as well, including glittery fabric fit for a prince or princess, lacey material for a bride's veil, and a cape for a super hero. Once you have the basics, continue to add to your trunk over the years. As your children get older, they may use the dress-up clothes in plays they create and perform for you.

Ann Vermel
San Francisco, CA

BEAUTY PARLOR

Curl up on the couch for an imaginary visit to the beauty parlor with your preschooler. Have combs, brushes, barrettes and hair elastics handy. Children love to play with hair, pretending to be a beautician. To add to the fun, call your child by your stylist's name. This activity can be expanded to applying lotion to mom's arms and legs. It's a fun activity for kids and certainly relaxing for moms.

Eileen Havey
Methuen, MA

SHOE STORE

This game began with my daughter's reluctance to try on shoes in the shoe store. I play the salesperson and she the customer. I measure her feet using a ruler and bring out various pairs of shoes (both hers and mine) for inspection and fitting. My daughter still does not love going to the store, but she no longer screams when the salesperson brings out the foot measure.

Ellen Zuckert
New York, NY

TRAIN RIDE

chairs	play money
hole punch	conductor's cap
paper scraps	rubber stamps

This idea came about on a rainy day when the kids were bored and wanted to go somewhere. We invented a pretend trip on a train to any place of their choice.

Begin by determining who will be the engineer, the conductor, the ticket seller, and the passengers. Line up several chairs in a row, one behind the other.

Each passenger buys a ticket from the ticket seller, who stamps the tickets with his rubber stamp. The conductor then yells "All aboard!" and the passengers board the train and choose seats. The conductor walks down the "aisle" punching tickets and collecting the stubs. The engineer is responsible for making sound effects and for yelling out the names of the stops. When all the passengers have disembarked at their destination, it is time to switch roles and start all over again.

Carol Siegel
Larchmont, NY

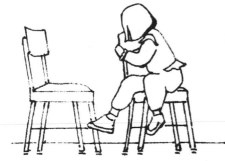

TENTING IN

On rainy days, our children love to take old sheets and towels and create a tent or playhouse inside. They hang the sheets over the kitchen table or drape them from a bed to a bureau or from one chair to another. Once the tent is created, the kids fill it with homemade beds, special toys, stuffed animals and kitchen gadgets. We enjoy reading stories together, having tea parties and sometimes a picnic lunch.

Sharon Hehn　　*Nancy Sullivan*
Chelmsford, MA　　*Andover, MA*

Ellen Zuckert
New York, NY

CAMPING

To occupy my children while I'm cooking dinner, I set up a pretend camp in the dining room. I close the blinds to darken the room. Then I bring out sleeping bags and flashlights. The kids love to get in and out of the sleeping bags and shine the flashlights on the ceiling. I even pull out a few plastic containers from our recycle bins and let my children "cook" dinner over a "campfire."

Bev Therkelsen
Andover, MA

BOX BONANZA

Wait! Don't throw away that box. Recycle it!

Use a tissue-sized box to make a small garage for toy cars. Be sure to leave the flaps on the garage doors. They provide half the fun.

Cut the top off of a medium-sized box. Then turn it over and cut two semi-circles on opposite sides to make a tunnel or bridge for toy cars.

Let your child decorate her boxed creations with crayons, markers, paints, or colored paper.

Nancy Singleton
N. Andover, MA

Becky Kangos
N. Andover, MA

COUPON CENTS

Many Sunday afternoons we use the newspaper for a fun game. First, the children cut out all the extra coupons. They then group them into piles according to value. For example, all the 50 cent coupons would be stacked together.

Next, I spread some coins on the floor and randomly choose one of the coupons. The children then have to find the right amount of change to match the coupon. They learn to recognize that 50 cents can be five dimes or two quarters, and so on.

After playing match up for a while, we move into the kitchen and play store. I ask what item they would like to buy and then pull it off the shelf. I tell them the cost and they have to figure out how many coins and coupons it will take to purchase the item. A calculator sometimes serves as the check-out register.

Deanna Espie
Andover, MA

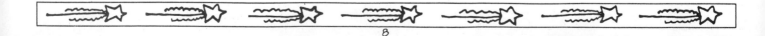

GROCERY SHOPPING

Children can't wait to do grown-up things, so this activity really captures their imaginations. Save empty food boxes and containers such as rice boxes, Cool Whip containers, milk containers, squeeze lemons, cereal boxes and pasta boxes. (Avoid any sharp or breakable containers.) Place the items on bookshelves or in "departments" around the room. Using play money, let your kids "grocery shop."

We bag in plastic or paper, just like a "real" store. It's a great way to recycle and an inexpensive way to have fun!

Susan Clark
Holderness, NH

PAPER BAG DRESS-UPS

When we were kids, Mom would keep us busy while she unpacked the groceries by letting us make costumes or masks out of paper grocery bags.

COSTUMES

Cut the bag up the back and then cut out a neck hole and armholes. Let your kids use crayons, paints, stickers or cut-up colored paper to decorate their costumes. Once they are wearing their costumes you can tape the back of the bag closed. My own children love to make armored suits and turtle shells with their bags.

MASKS

Cut out armholes and eye-holes and then let your kids decorate the masks. I loved pretending to be an animal or a monster from outer space.

Nancy Burnham
N. Andover, MA

Cindy Brown
Andover, MA

MAKING PRETEND SOUP

large bowl	measuring cups
small bowl	spices
wooden spoon	

This is a great way to occupy your child while you are working in the kitchen.

Fill a large bowl half full of water. (It can be placed in the sink to avoid any mess.) Give your child some old spices to add to the water and a wooden spoon for mixing after each addition.

When the soup is "done," your child can use the measuring cup to scoop some soup into a smaller bowl. He may spend a lot of time dumping and re-serving his creation.

Barbara Weiss
N. Andover, MA

Helen McKnight
Andover, MA

PRETEND RESTAURANT

Help your child write out a pretend menu. Then lay out a blanket on the floor for a tablecloth and let your child set the table with plates, cups and cutlery. Take turns playing waiter and customer. A friend tells me that she taught her nieces some table etiquette this way!

Ellen Zuckert
New York, NY

YOUR SUPER CHILD

Transform your child into a hero(ine) by making a cape out of a colorful towel. Wrap two corners around your child's shoulders and join the corners together with a rubberband. Your super child is now ready to leap into action.

Variation: Cut a "V" shape in the shorter end of an old "baby towel" and tie the towel around your child's neck to make a cape. Then use stickers to personalize the hero's cape. You might also cut out masks from felt squares.

Norma Villarreal   *Ann Geary*
Andover, MA   *Andover, MA*

WEATHER DRESS-UP

To make my two-year-old daughter more aware of the seasons and different types of weather, we play a dress-up game. I ask her "What shall we wear if it's hot and sunny?" She then finds a pair of sunglasses and a bathing suit. We also talk about activities we might do on this type of day, such as going to the beach and making sandcastles. Then we find clothes to wear if the weather turns rainy or snowy. The first thing my daughter now asks when she wakes up in the morning is, "What kind of day is it?"

Wendy Venti
N. Andover, MA

THIRSTY COWHANDS

To encourage us to drink water, my mother used to offer us water from a soup ladle. It always tasted better that way and in western movies that was how cowboys drank their water. In the summer, you can fill a clean bucket and have your own watering hole.

Susan Richardson
Andover, MA

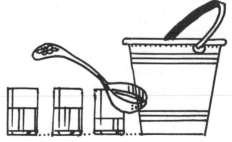

TEDDY BEAR COSTUMES

My five-year-old's bear, Gundi, has been my son's best friend for years and continues to be a springboard for his imagination and creativity. Using colored construction paper, scissors, crayons, and tape, he creates costumes or hats for Gundi and then enjoys playing with "Super Bear" or whomever the bear has become. The paper apparel is quite temporary yet provides him with a new personality for the day and gives me some "golden minutes."

Bobbie Lantow
Andover, MA

FLASHLIGHT TEDDY

Hide a few bears in a selected area of the house while your children are in another room. Then turn off the lights, give the children flashlights and let them find the bears. Your children may also want to have a turn hiding the bears for Mom and Dad to find.

Sharon Hehn
Chelmsford, MA

PAPER DOLL GLOBETROTTERS

When I was young, my sisters and I used to spend many an afternoon traveling around the world with paper dolls. We decided where to go by spinning the globe. We'd close our eyes and one of us would touch the globe. Then we'd all look to see where the finger had landed. If it had landed on Brazil, for example, we would look up "International Costumes" in the encyclopedia to see what people in Brazil might wear.

Next we would design clothes for our trip to Brazil, including a travel outfit, beach wear, and, of course, an elegant evening dress. (Be sure to draw tabs on all the clothes.)

There are other possibilities as well: tracing or drawing the country and marking the places your doll will be visiting, or drawing the kind of house she might live in if she grew up in that country.

Mary Pritchard
Andover, MA

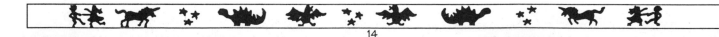

STORYTELLING

Each of my children has her own notebook and at least once a week they dictate a story to me. I write down what they say (whether it makes sense or not) and then read their stories aloud once they've finished. They enjoy listening to each other's stories and "re-reading" old stories. It's fascinating to see how the content and complexity of their stories has changed over time.

Elizabeth Fletcher Foy
N. Andover, MA

STORY GAME

This is a fantasy activity involving the whole family.

Put the names of characters from a familiar folktale, fairytale or favorite book into a bag. Each member of the family pulls out a character card. Then the whole family acts out the story with each member staying in character.

A more open-ended version of this activity is to make up your own character, setting and action cards. Put each category of card into a separate bag. Each family member selects a character card. Then someone selects a setting card and an action card and reads the cards aloud to the group. The object of the game is for the characters to work together to overcome the problem suggested by the action card. Play ends once this conflict is resolved.

For example, three players might select "King," "Dragon," and "Eagle" from the character-card bag. The setting card selected might read "beach" and the action card "raining." The characters develop the plot from there. Save your character, setting and action cards for further play!

Jo-Ann Wangh
Stow, MA

LETTER FUN

My husband and daughter play a game on the computer involving letters. First, my three-year-old daughter dictates a letter to her dad and he enters it on the keyboard. Then my husband dictates a letter to my daughter and she pretends to enter his letter. This activity spurs creativity by reinforcing storytelling.

<u>VARIATION:</u> I often let my four-year-old play with the typewriter on indoor days. He has fun creating "messages" on the paper and the activity stimulates letter and number recognition.

Susan Bourland
Andover, MA

Pat Picard
Andover, MA

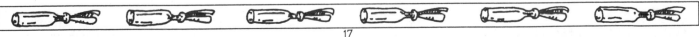

A DAY AT THE OCEAN

Every February or March my play group gets together for a day at the ocean. We create the beach on our kitchen floor by spreading a large piece of plastic on the floor and placing a small plastic sand box filled with sand in the middle. Everyone brings additional beach paraphernalia to the party including shells, seaweed, cassette tapes with "ocean" sounds, beach chairs, pails and shovels. We turn up the thermostat and get into our bathing suits. We sip virgin frozen piña colada drinks and eat popsicles and fudgesicles.

Donna Kane
Lawrence, MA

LAUNDRY BASKET BOATING

A laundry basket makes a wonderful boat. It's fun to sing "Sailing, Sailing, Over The Bounding Sea," or "Row, Row, Row Your Boat," as your children rock back and forth in their boat.

Carly Therkelsen
Andover, MA

MAGIC ROCKS

Have everyone, adults and children alike, crouch down on the floor, curl up in a small ball, and become a "Magic Rock."

Then have someone call out "Magic Rocks, Magic Rocks turn into a _____" and fill in the blank with a word of her choice. It can be an animal, insect, or object.

As soon as the last word is spoken, everyone becomes that animal or object by moving and making the appropriate sounds. For example, if "Bird" is called out, you might stand up and flap your arms as you run around the room chirping.

After thirty seconds or so, have an adult call out "Magic Rocks!" and everyone becomes a rock again. Repeat the game as many times as you like.

Catherine Fletcher
Chicago, IL

POW-WOW

This is a great way to encourage organization and neatness. Sit crosslegged with your child and smoke a pretend peace pipe (a pencil or marker will do). Look around the room and discuss where things belong. After you have verbally agreed where everything belongs, get up and organize the room together. When you have finished, sit down to smoke the peace pipe again and admire the neat room.

Linda Francalancia-Hacker
Andover, MA

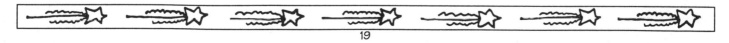

TREASURE HUNT

On mornings when my daughter is reluctant to get out of her cozy bed, I use a treasure hunt to entice her. I create a clue using a picture of a household object, such as a toaster oven. She finds another picture clue at the toaster oven which leads her somewhere else. She continues to find picture clues until she reaches the treasure, which could be a small cereal box or a stick of gum. It always works!

Deborah Spaulding
Manhattan Beach, CA

I play a game with my daughter which encourages teeth brushing. First she pretends she is the mommy and brushes my teeth. Then she lets me be the mom and brush her teeth.

Susan Bourland
Andover, MA

Recently my two children rediscovered their old Halloween costumes. Their role playing kept them busy for a surprisingly long period of time.

Marcia S. Mucci
Methuen, MA

When teaching your preschooler to pretend with the telephone, teach her to dial the local emergency number or 911 if your town has that service.

Sharon Thies
Andover, MA

Make dinner special by turning off the lights and eating by candlelight. If you have a fireplace, it is fun to make a fire and set the table in front of it. The kids feel like they are having dinner at a special restaurant.

Jodi Templer
Tewksbury, MA

Encourage your child's natural interest in her family history by playing "This Is Your Life." Assist her in interviewing grandparents, aunts, and uncles on a camcorder or tape recorder. Have her ask them to tell her a scary, funny, or silly story that happened to them. Our children love to hear stories about things that "really" happened and how we resolved the situation.

Nancy Chandler
N. Andover, MA

If you animate an object, such as a favorite doll, stuffed animal, or even a flashlight, you and the object may be able to convince your child to complete a task. My daughter will listen to her Madeline doll begging her to get dressed and play with her much sooner than she will listen to me saying the same thing.

Michele Maldari
Andover, MA

Help your child create her own treasure island map. Make a key with symbols for mountains, rivers, lakes, and beaches. You can make the map look old by crumpling it up and then dipping its edges in tea or burning its corners.

Andrew Fletcher
New York, NY

Flannel boards are a great way to encourage storytelling and make-believe. You can get a flannel board and a kit of felt shapes and figures at a school supply store. Then take turns telling stories with your child using the shapes and figures. Buy pieces of felt and make your own characters to include in your stories.

Paula Movsesian
Andover, MA

Record your children's special performances, plays, and puppet shows on a video tape reserved just for that purpose. Children love to watch movies of themselves and the videos will be a keepsake for them in later years.

Bev Therkelsen
Andover, MA

For a light lunch on play group day, my children and I sometimes use cookie cutters to cut bologna and cheese or PB & J sandwiches into kooky shapes. They are much more fun to eat this way!

Marcia Strykowski   Karen Sloan
Bradford, MA   Plainview, NY

ART PROJECTS

SCRIBBLE COOKIES

muffin tin	muffin cups
peeled crayons	

Save broken crayons to make scribble cookies. Use a knife to cut the crayons into small bits. Line a muffin tray with paper muffin cups and fill them approximately one third full with the crayon bits. Preheat the oven to 300° F. Place the filled muffin tin in the oven and immediately turn off the heat. Once the crayon bits have melted, remove the tray from the oven and allow the crayon cookies to harden. Peel off the paper cups and the rainbow scribble cookies are ready to use!

Marcia S. Mucci
Methuen, MA

Sylvia Stephenson
Deedee Roberts
Family Cooperative Preschool
N. Andover, MA

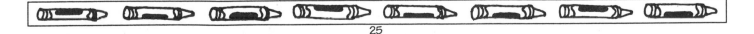

25

MARBLE PAINTING

marbles	white paper
tempera paint	cookie sheet

Pour different colors of paint into separate bowls and drop a marble into each bowl. Place a sheet of white paper in a container with sides, such as a box or cookie sheet. Place the paint-covered marbles on the paper and tilt the box from side to side allowing the marbles to roll back and forth across the paper. Your children will enjoy watching the marbles make patterns of paint trails.

Sheila Torrisi
Methuen, MA

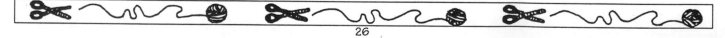

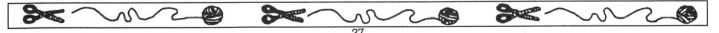

BUILD A RECYCLED CITY

glue	small boxes
paint	paintbrushes
scissors	paper recyclables
cardboard	plastic recyclables

For weeks, my oldest daughter, Sarah, industriously saved toilet paper rolls, plastic bottles, popsicle sticks, party hats, cereal boxes, yarn, and more to make a city. Getting caught up in the excitement, her sister, Katie, started her own collection of trash. When they had collected enough things they asked for glue, scissors, paint and paintbrushes. Using a piece of heavy cardboard as a base, they constructed and painted their cities.

Elizabeth Fletcher Foy
N. Andover, MA

EGGSHELL MOSAIC

paper	paint/paintbrush
eggshells	glue

Wash discarded eggshells and let them dry. Put the dried shells in a ziplocked plastic bag and let your child crush them into large and medium chunks. Using a paintbrush, have your child spread a thin layer of glue onto a piece of paper. Then let her sprinkle the eggshell chunks onto the paper. You can use cookie cutters or stencils to help define shapes. After the glue has dried, let your child paint her mosaic.

Patti Meade
Andover, MA

POPSICLE STICK PUZZLE

popsicle sticks   markers
masking tape

Lay 10 popsicle sticks side by side on a flat surface. Place a piece of masking tape across the back of the popsicle sticks to hold them together. Then flip them over and let your child draw a picture on the wooden surface. When he has finished, remove the tape from the back side. Mix up the sticks and challenge your child to put his puzzle back together.

Kathy Meade
Dorchester, MA

SPIDER PAINTING

5 pipe cleaners   paper
aluminum foil tray   paint

Children will be captivated by the thought of painting with a spider. Twist four pipe cleaners together to form a spider with its eight legs. Use the fifth pipe cleaner to make a handle.

Pour paint into an aluminum foil tray. Let your child paint with the spider by dipping its legs in the paint and then dabbing the spider on paper. Provide your child with different colors of paint so that she can make colorful designs with her spider.

Lucia Carelli
Methuen, MA

BUBBLE PAINTING

water	tempera paint
paper	Lemon Joy detergent
straws	
coffee tins	

Fill a coffee tin with 1/4 cup of Lemon Joy detergent and 1/2 cup of water. Add some paint for color and stir the solution well. The more paint you add, the brighter the prints.

Give your child a straw and have him blow gently through the straw until bubbles begin to overflow from the container. To produce the best bubbles, don't let the straw touch the bottom of the container when blowing.

(Caution: Make sure your child blows through the straw and does not suck.)

Once bubbles begin to overflow from the coffee can, press a sheet of paper on the bubbles by laying the paper across the rim of the can. Remove the sheet of paper and press it against a new can containing bubbles of a different color. Repeat these steps using as many different colors as you like.

Kate Anderson
Community Cooperative
Nursery School
N. Andover, MA

BATH TOWEL SPLAT MATS

Splat mats are easy to make and can be used under messy activities, high chairs, or dog bowls.

Place an old bath towel on top of some newspaper to protect your floor. Have your child stand over the towel and squirt fabric paints on one half of the towel. Then fold the towel in half so the design makes a mirror image. Open up the towel and let it dry. Your splat mat may be stiff at first but it will soften up after being washed.

Susan Ickes
Andover, MA

EGG CARTON TYPEWRITER

glue/stapler	number stickers
egg carton	paper towel roll
letter stickers	construction paper

Open an egg carton and turn it upside down. Place a sheet of construction paper in the middle of the upside down carton between its top and bottom. Place a cardboard tube horizontally behind the construction paper and then glue or staple the paper and tube together. Attach this unit to the egg carton using a stapler or glue. Let your child stick number and letter stickers on top of the egg holders to make the keys of the typewriter. Your child may now type as many imaginary stories or letters as she likes.

Ethel Schuster
Andover, MA

EGG CARTON CATERPILLARS

glue	egg carton
paint	pipe cleaners
buttons	paint brushes

Cut an egg carton in half lengthwise. Let your child paint each of the egg carton strips. As soon as they are dry, your child can decorate the strips using buttons for eyes and pipe cleaners for the antennae and mouth. Follow up this activity by talking about how caterpillars become butterflies or read a story about caterpillars.

Patty O'Connor
Community Day Care Center
Lawrence, MA

EGG CARTON TULIPS

egg cartons	paint or markers
pipe cleaners	colored beads

These flowers will brighten up your house even on the coldest winter day. Paint one or two egg cartons in bright multi-colors.

An adult should puncture the bottom of each egg-holder and then cut the cartons into individual "flowers." Have your child insert a pipe cleaner through the base of each flower. Then thread a bead onto both ends of each pipe cleaner. Position each flower on its stem by adjusting the beads. Several flowers together make a beautiful bouquet.

Nancy Lewis-Schulz
N. Andover, MA

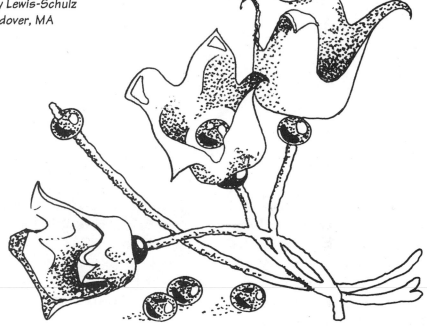

31

HOMEMADE HAND PRINT

1 c. salt	2 c. flour
1/2 c. water	2 Tbl. veg. oil

A homemade hand print makes an excellent gift for Mother's Day or Father's Day.

Mix the salt, water, and oil together in a large bowl. Then add the flour and knead the mixture well to remove any air bubbles. Form part of the clay into a softball-sized ball. Use a rolling pin to flatten the ball into a slab of uniform thickness. Press your child's hand into the clay slab to form a hand print. Then place the slab on a cookie sheet and bake it at 250° F for several hours.

After it has cooled, outline your child's hand print with a marker. Then label the slab with your child's name and the date the print was made.

VARIATION: Mix plaster of Paris according to the directions on the box. Then pour it into a 6 1/2-inch pie pan. When the plaster reaches the right consistency--not too sticky and not too hard--quickly press your child's hand onto its surface. Once dry, let your child paint her hand print. Then finish with a layer of urethane to prevent the paint from peeling.

Cheryl Torres *Sylvia Stephenson*
Methuen, MA *N. Andover, MA*

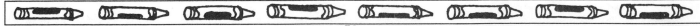

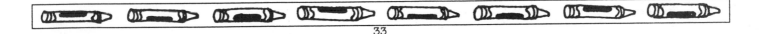

PLAY DOUGH

1 c. flour	2 Tbl. Cream of Tartar
1 c. water	1 envelope Kool-Aid
1/4 c. salt	(unsweetened, not grape)
1 Tbl. veg. oil	or food coloring

In a saucepan, mix all of the dry ingredients except the Kool-Aid. In a small bowl, mix the water and the Kool-Aid or food coloring. Add the colored water and the oil to the dry ingredients. Stir the mixture over medium heat for 3 to 5 minutes, until the dough forms a ball in the pan. Knead the ball on a floured surface for one minute. Once the play dough has cooled, it is ready to use. If you store your play dough in an airtight container, it should last for several weeks.

Mary Jo Melloni
Tewksbury, MA

Denise Goudreault
Haverhill, MA

Lucia Carelli
Methuen, MA

Sandy Kingsland
Scituate, MA

STAINED GLASS FIGURES

glue	tape
wax paper	scissors
food coloring	paper cups
paintbrushes	cookie sheet

Pour glue into several small paper cups and color it with food coloring. Place a piece of wax paper on a cookie sheet and hold it in place with tape. Using a paintbrush, have your child spread a thin and even layer of the different colored glues onto the wax paper. Once your child has finished, place a second piece of wax paper on top of the painted piece. Let the glue dry and then cut the wax paper into shapes or favorite figures and hang them in a window.

Patty O'Connor
Community Day Care Center
Lawrence, MA

STAINED GLASS LETTERS

crayons	paintbrush
white paper	watercolors

Print your child's name in block letters on a sheet of lightweight paper, such as airmail or typing paper. Using crayons, let your child draw pictures or patterns inside the letters. Then have him paint the letters using watercolors. The watercolor will resist the crayon and be absorbed only by the white areas. When your child has finished, cut out his name and hang it in a window.

Luci Prawdzik
Andover, MA

RAINBOW SALT JARS

glue	glass jar
salt	colored chalk
funnel	styrofoam trays

Pour some salt onto a styrofoam tray. Color the salt by rubbing a piece of colored chalk back and forth through the salt. Using a funnel, pour the colored salt into a glass container. (Baby food jars work well.) Continue adding layers of different colored salt until the container is filled. Tip the container as you fill it to make hills and valleys. If your container does not have a cover, put a layer of household glue on top to hold the salt in place.

Maureen MacRae
Andover, MA

Lynne Doxsey
Andover, MA

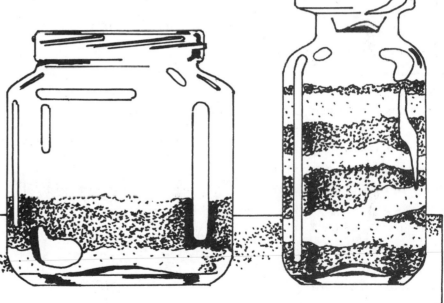

DESIGNER PILLOWCASES

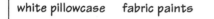

white pillowcase   fabric paints

This project is a great party activity. Lay a pillowcase on top of a dropcloth or outside on the grass. Using fabric paint, let your child paint a design, or simply splatter paint, on the pillowcase. When the paint is dry, turn the pillowcase over and let your child decorate its other side. When both sides are completely dry, put a pillow in the pillowcase and place it on your child's bed.

Sharon Thies
Andover, MA

DESIGNER PLACEMATS

glue	contact paper
paper	collage materials
scissors	drawing materials

Make the dinner table a bright and creative place by setting it with placemats your children have made. Invite your child to draw or paint a favorite picture on a piece of paper. If your child is old enough, encourage her to design a placemat for each family member that highlights a special interest of that individual. For example, if Nana is a birdwatcher, your child might draw birds on her placemat. If Dad is a Celtics fan, his placemat might have basketballs on it. To spur on creativity, supply your artist with collage materials, such as fabric scraps, glitter, and old magazines.

Protect the finished placemats from spills by placing them between two sheets of clear contact paper. Your child can now have fun setting the table and letting the diners guess where they sit.

Donald Price
Tewksbury, MA

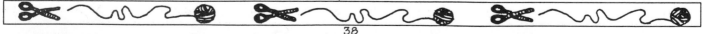

CLOTH BUTTON POCKET

chalk	needle and thread
button	cotton fabric - 1 sq. ft.
scissors	

I remember making this cloth button pocket when I was in first grade at Shawsheen School some 30 years ago. My teacher used it as a Kleenex or hanky holder.

Using a piece of chalk, trace the outline of a house on the cotton fabric. Then trace and cut out a square shape that is the same size as the base of the house. (See illustration.) Sew three sides of the square piece of cloth to the base of the house, leaving its top side open.

Cut a button hole-size slit in the roof of the house. Now sew a button in the middle of the square shape and fold over the roof flap to button the pocket closed.

Susan McKelliget
Andover, MA

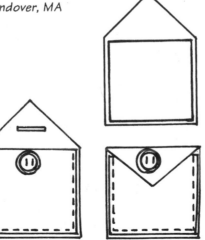

BUTTON FLOWERS

glue	pipe cleaners
buttons	construction paper

Draw an outline of a flower pot on a piece of construction paper. Cut out the flower pot shape and glue it onto a piece of construction paper.

Make flower stems using pipe cleaners. Have your child glue the pipe cleaners onto the construction paper as if they are sprouting out of the flower pot. Then let your child arrange some buttons into a flower shape and glue them above each stem.

Beth Prawdzik
Andover, MA

KEEPSAKE BOX

glue	shoe box
scissors	fabric scraps

Invite your child to rummage through your fabric scraps and select some pieces that appeal to her. Your child can cut the scraps into geometric shapes and glue the pieces onto the top of a shoe box. Cover its entire surface to give the box top a patchwork quilt-look.

Cover the base of the box in a similar manner or cut one piece of fabric to fit each side and glue these pieces in place. The solid pieces of fabric provide a nice contrast to the multicolored top. (Let your child help you measure the sides.)

Use the quilted box to hold crayons, jewelry, doll clothes, or little people.

Mary Pritchard
Andover, MA

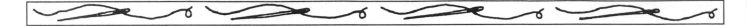

BEAN BAGS

fabric paint	needle and thread
sturdy fabric	split peas/uncooked rice

Cut two 3 1/2 inch by 5 inch rectangles out of a sturdy piece of fabric. Lay one of the rectangles on top of the other and sew three of their sides together using a tight stitch. Turn the fabric bag inside out and have your children fill the bags with approximately 1/3 cup of split peas and/or uncooked rice. Then stitch the fourth side of the bean bag closed.

If you use white fabric your children can decorate or personalize their bags with fabric paint before filling them with beans. Then after the fabric paint dries completely, fill and stitch their bean bags closed.

If you use three different colored pieces of fabric, younger children can play a sorting game with their bean bags. Make two bean bags out of each color, producing a total of six bean bags. Put three different colored bean bags in a bowl and place the three matching bean bags on the floor. Let your child match the colors in the bowl with those on the floor.

You can also use these bean bags to play a tossing game. Have your children stand a set distance away from a bucket and try to "make a basket" with their bean bags.

Sharon Thies
Andover, MA

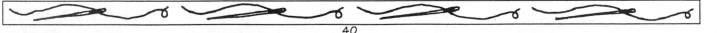

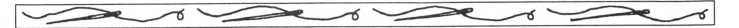

EASY WEAVING

yarn	scissors
shoe box	hole punch

My children got on a weaving kick, but instead of buying a loom we made our own.

Using a hole punch, make evenly spaced holes along the sides of a shoe box, with the same number of holes on opposite sides. (The closer the holes, the tighter the weave.)

Tie regular weight yarn across the loom lengthwise to form the warp. To make it easier to lift off the finished product, make the warp using one long piece of yarn. Weave the yarn back and forth through the holes until you have created five to six (more if you are weaving a wider piece) lines running the length of the shoe box. (See diagram.) Tie very heavy yarn (approximately 1/4 inch by 1/2 inch thickness) to the bottom right hole on the long side of the shoe box. Show your child how to weave by threading the yarn over and under the warp which runs lengthwise.

Before removing the finished product from the loom, tie any loose ends to the weaving to prevent unraveling. Then cut through the cardboard at each hole and simply lift the weaving off of the loom. My children have woven little scarves and tiny rugs for their stuffed animals and pot holders for the kitchen. Even my ten-year-old son enjoyed this activity!

For a more permanent frame, nail four pieces of wood together into a square or rectangle shape. Then hammer evenly spaced nails along the wood, leaving 1/8 inch of the nail sticking up out of the frame.

Jodi Templer
Tewksbury, MA

DECORATIVE COAT HOOK

paint	3/4 in. x 4 in. board
screws	3 in. clothes hook
rosettes	carpenter's glue
wood molding	window corners

A decorative coat hook is a woodworking project that the entire family can enjoy making.

Visit a lumber supply store to select various decorative moldings, rosettes, window corners, or wooden shapes. You may create a wooden coat hook of any length using any combination of decorative wooden pieces. The following instructions are according to a coat hook we designed.

Saw a 3/4-inch board and a piece of molding into 14-inch lengths. Let your children paint the various pieces of wood (the window corners are especially fun to paint) using contrasting colors.

Using carpenter's glue, glue the painted molding to the top 3/4 inch edge of the board. Make sure the molding edge is flush with the back of the board so that the board will lie flat against the wall when it is hung. Glue the rosettes or window corners onto each end of the front of the board. Then cut a piece of molding to fit along the front of the board between the window corners and just beneath the top piece of molding. Glue it in place. Position a clothes hook in the center of the board and screw it in place.

The Herhold/Wondolowski Family
Swampscott, MA

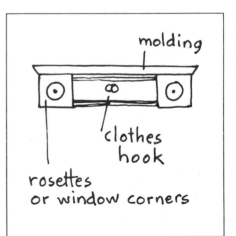

molding

clothes hook

rosettes or window corners

TISSUE PAPER BRACELET

glue	tissue paper
stapler	poster board

Cut a piece of poster board into long strips that are approximately one inch wide. Then cut colored tissue paper into strips of different lengths and widths. Let your child spread glue on both sides of the poster board strip and begin wrapping tissue paper around the strip. When she has finished, staple or tape the ends of the poster board strip together to fit around your child's wrist.

Mary Jo Melloni
Tewksbury, MA

WRAPPING PAPER NECKLACE

glue	wrapping paper
scissors	4 toilet paper rolls
wide ribbon	paint/markers/crayons

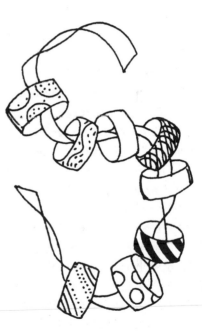

This is an easy necklace for young children to make. Cut each toilet paper roll into three rings. Let your child decorate the rings by gluing wrapping paper around them or using paint, markers, or crayons. Give your child a 20-inch strip of wide ribbon and let her string the rings onto the ribbon. When she has finished, tie the ribbon to make a necklace.

Diane Paff
Andover, MA

SKINNIES

glue	magazines
scissors	poster board
catalogs	

I grew up in a household of seven girls and can remember the fun we used to have making "skinnies," a cousin to the paper doll. The big Sears catalog was a good source for our skinnies' wardrobes.

Make an entire family of skinnies by cutting out strips of poster board, approximately nine inches long and one inch wide. To complete the figures, cut out heads and feet from the poster board and glue them onto the strips, or draw them on before cutting out the strips. Then go through clothing catalogs, cut out clothes (including arms), and dress your skinnies by gluing on the outfits.

Mary Jo Melloni
Tewksbury, MA

WALLPAPER BOOKS

wallpaper	needle
cardboard	wide colored tape
white paper	spray adhesive glue
dental floss	

These books are fun to make and ideal for recording stories or diary entries, or storing family pictures and drawings. They also make a nice gift for friends or family.

Cut two 9 by 12 inch pieces of cardboard. Then cut two 11 by 14 inch pieces of wallpaper or fabric. Place the wallpaper pieces, non-patterned side up, on newspaper and spray them with spray adhesive glue.

Quickly, have your child center each piece of cardboard on top of the sticky non-patterned side of the wallpaper. Together, fold over the overlapping edges of the wallpaper. Press down hard so that the wallpaper will adhere to the cardboard. You should now have two equally sized pieces of wallpaper-covered cardboard.

Next fold six to ten pieces of 11 by 16 inch white paper in half. Thread dental floss through a needle and tie a knot in one end. Bind the book by sewing the pages together at the fold. Make stitches about every inch.

Cut a 14-inch strip of wide colored tape and lay it sticky side up on the table. Place the long edges of each cardboard cover on top of the tape to resemble a book. Leave about 1/2 inch of the sticky tape exposed between the cardboard so the bound pages can be attached. Place the bound pages between the two cardboard covers and press the pages against the tape with your hand. Glue the first and last page of the book to the front and back cardboard pieces, respectively. Fold over the two ends of colored tape to hold down the pieces of paper that are glued to the front and back cover. The folded ends of the tape should be under the other pages. Your book is now ready to use!

NOTE: To make smaller books, use 6 by 8 inch pieces of cardboard, 7 by 9 inch pieces of wallpaper, and 8 1/2 by 11 inch white paper.

Nancy Maher
Andover, MA

PUPPET-IN-A-CUP

straws	glue
paper cups	scissors
magazines	paints/crayons

Draw a face on a piece of paper or cut one out from a magazine. Tape the picture onto one end of a straw. Punch a hole in the bottom of a paper cup and, holding the cup upside down, place the other end of the straw through the hole. Let your child decorate and clothe her puppet using paints or crayons. For added fun, give your child fabric scraps and other collage materials with which to dress her puppet.

Cricket's Classroom
Community Day Care Center
Lawrence, MA

SOCK PUPPETS

I remember making sock puppets when I was a child, so the idea is probably as old as the history of socks! Insert your hand into an outgrown sock to identify the best spot for a face. Take off the sock and let your child decorate the puppet with markers. Then glue on art materials to create a puppet face. When the glue has dried, the puppet is ready to perform in a puppet show.

Marcia Mucci
Methuen, MA

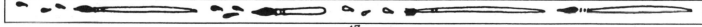

JAPANESE FISH KITE

string	glue
cereal box	stapler
tissue paper	scissors
pens/markers	hole punch

A Japanese kite is unique, in part, because it has a bridle to hold or fly it by.

To make the bridle, cut a 1 by 20 inch strip from a large, empty cereal box or from poster board. Staple the ends of the strip together, forming a ring with an 18-inch circumference. Using a hole punch, make four equidistant holes around the ring. Tie four pieces of string to each of the holes. The pieces of string should be at least seven inches long after they have been tied onto the bridle so that they meet in the middle and can be tied together. Once you have tied the four pieces of string together, tie another piece of string at this juncture. You will use this string later to fly the kite.

To make the fish, fold a large piece of tissue paper lengthwise to make a 10 by 25 inch rectangle. Decorate both sides of the fish imaginatively. Draw the gills, eyes, scales and tail onto both sides of this rectangle. Then cut one end of the rectangle into strips to make a tail. Children may need to see pictures of fish for decorative ideas. When the fish is completely decorated, glue its mouth to the bridle. Then form its body into a tube by gluing the long edges of its tissue-paper body together. Your kite is now ready to fly!

Mimi Cole
Woodlands, TX

DECORATIVE KITE

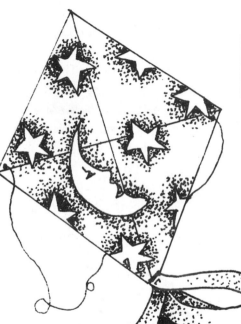

markers	string
crayons	stapler
poster board	crepe paper

Cut a piece of poster board or heavy construction paper into a large diamond shape that resembles a kite. Let your child decorate the kite using markers or crayons. Make a tail from colorful crepe paper and staple it to the kite. Cut two pieces of string and staple the two pieces to opposite sides of the kite. Tie the two pieces of string together and then hang the kite from the ceiling. Your child will enjoy watching her kite blow in the wind!

Nancy Maher
Andover, MA

FELT FLAGS

paper	felt squares
glitter	popsicle sticks
stars	rickrack

We enjoy making felt flags to decorate our house. Begin by cutting colored felt squares into 3 by 5 inch pieces. Decorate the felt flag and the stick with glitter, rickrack, strips of paper, and stars. Glue one end of the felt square to a large popsicle stick, which you can find in craft stores.

Encourage your child to learn about the flags of other countries by copying their designs from the encyclopedia. Then encourage your child to design a flag for an imaginary place.

Susan Ickes
Andover, MA

Soon after our daughter started nursery school, she began bringing home bagfuls of artwork. She was reluctant to throw anything away and we were quickly outgrowing display and storage space. Then I hit upon the idea of videotaping our daughter each week describing her latest works of art. My daughter loved the idea and has since had lots of fun presenting her artwork to the camera.

Peter Beatty
Andover, MA

Keep a large box, oversized envelope, or portfolio for all of your children's artwork. Be sure to mark their names and the date on each piece of artwork.

Jenny Bixby
Acton, MA

Skin So Soft by Avon works wonders in removing stickers on clothing that has gone through the wash. Just dab a little Skin So Soft on the problem area and then wash the clothing immediately to avoid staining.

Diane Sousa
Newton, NH

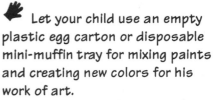

Let your child use an empty plastic egg carton or disposable mini-muffin tray for mixing paints and creating new colors for his work of art.

Sue Siegel
Andover, MA

To help children learn how to use scissors, draw three lines on a piece of paper, approximately two inches apart. Make each line three inches long and at the end of each line draw an X. Have your child cut along each line until he reaches the X.

Bev Therkelsen
Andover, MA

I always save wrapping paper and tin foil tubes for multiple purposes. We use smaller tubes for trumpets in an impromptu band, tunnels for matchbox cars, or telescopes for spying on buddies. We use larger tubes for transporting special artwork made at school or a friend's house. Simply roll up the artwork and carefully insert it into the tube for protection.

Sue Siegel
Andover, MA

Use hair spray to remove ballpoint pen and marker from clothing, upholstery, and furniture surfaces. Test a small, hidden area first to be sure the spray won't ruin the fabric or furniture finish. Then spray the mark with a small amount of hair spray. Leave it for a few minutes and then wash or wipe off the excess.

Patti Meade
Andover, MA

Use a damp sponge and baking soda paste to remove "artwork" from your walls. I've removed crayon, pencil, and even ball-point pen this way.

Jane Cairns
Andover, MA

One of my favorite summer events when I was a child, was a kid's art show held in our neighborhood. Artwork was grouped by age and type of media (for example, crayons, watercolors, or oil) and displayed along the fence and trees in someone's backyard. All participants received ribbons at the end of the show.

Catherine Fletcher
Chicago, IL

For a change of pace, let your child paint outside on his easel, or lay a roll of newsprint on the ground and let him finger paint. Keep a hose handy for clean up.

Sue Siegel
Andover, MA

OUTDOOR
FUN

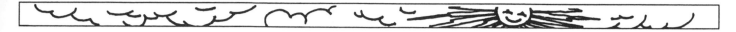

SKY WATCHING

One of my favorite activities comes after a period of active play. My sons and I lie flat on our backs in our backyard and talk about the sky and clouds. We look for shapes of animals or objects in the clouds and imagine what those animals or objects are doing.

It is a good way to get my sons to slow down and use their imaginations.   Lying on our backs, staring up at the sky, is also a relaxing way to bring up something important I have been meaning to discuss with my children.

Carolyn Cameron
Phoenix, AZ

BIG SOAP BUBBLES

6 c. water
3/4 c. white Karo syrup
2 c. Lemon Joy detergent

Combine all of the above ingredients in a covered container. Shake the mixture vigorously for 30 seconds and then place it in the refrigerator to settle for four hours.

Remove the mixture and let it warm to room temperature. Then pour it into a shallow pan and give each child a plastic children's clothes hanger to make huge bubbles.

Wendy Barry
Andover, MA

Denise Iozzo
Reading, MA

CAR WASH

soap   sponges
bucket   plastic riding toys

Give your child a bucket filled with soapy water and some sponges and let her wash her plastic riding toys, or any other plastic toys that need a cleaning. My three-year-old loves to scrub down her toys and the toys get clean in the process!

Jill McLaughlin
Andover, MA

SUPER SQUIRTERS

> hammer and nail
> 2-liter plastic soda bottles

That bag of recyclable plastic two-liter soda bottles down in the basement came in awfully handy the day of my son's ninth birthday party. The outdoor thermometer shot up to 95° F and all the kids wanted to do was run around and get wet! We didn't have enough water guns to go around, so my eldest son thought of recycling the soda bottles as water squirters!

Using a hammer and nail, we made a hole in the plastic cap of each bottle. Then we filled the bottles with water, screwed on the tops, and they were ready to squirt. All the remaining party games involved water fun. We squirted specific targets as part of a relay race, did some long distance squirting, and played squirt the members of the other team.

Karen M. Sloan
Plainview, NY

WATER PAINTING

Give your child a bucket of water and a large paintbrush and let him paint the house, the sidewalk, the car, the fence, or whatever else may be around your house.

Shelley Selwyn   *Nancy Laorenza*
Andover, MA   *N. Andover, MA*

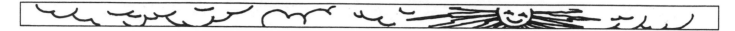

CHALK CIRCLE GAME

When the children are charging madly about the house, I grab a piece of chalk and herd them outdoors to play this game.

Using chalk, draw a convoluted path of circles on the pavement that eventually circles back to the first circle. Draw the circles large enough to accommodate two kid-size feet. The spacing of the circles depends on the ages of your children.

Mark a start circle and have your children hop from one circle to another all the way around the track. The more circles you draw, the more exhausted your children will be at the end of this game.

After we play this game, the girls shuffle back inside and sit down quietly to draw.

Elizabeth Fletcher Foy
N. Andover, MA

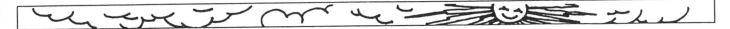

RIDE-ON PARADE

Have children bring their favorite ride-on toy to play group. Then line up the children on their ride-on toys and have an adult or child lead the parade.

<u>VARIATION:</u> To add to the fun, make an obstacle course for the children to negotiate. The course might include chairs to ride around, a tunnel—made from a blanket stretched across two chairs—to ride through, and a ramp on which to ride up and down.

Shelley Selwyn
Andover, MA

DRIVEWAY ROAD MAPS

For a really big chalkboard, use your driveway! Children can draw streets and then add local points of interest, such as the post office, the fire station, the supermarket, and Grandma's house. Don't let them forget to add their own house and some railroad tracks. An imaginary train can chug around town doing errands.

<u>VARIATION:</u> Use colored sidewalk chalk to draw huge pictures that take up the entire driveway. Two of our favorite pictures are of enormous dragons and gigantic school buses.

Marcia Strykowski   *Gail Zwerling*
Bradford, MA   *Andover, MA*

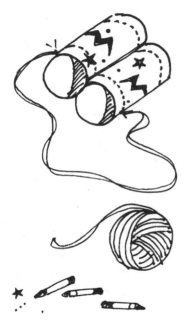

SAFARI BINOCULARS

foil	stickers
tape	markers
yarn	2 toilet paper rolls
crayons	construction paper
cellophane	

These binoculars are easy to make and inspire hours of imaginative play. Tape two toilet paper rolls together and let your child decorate her binoculars using crayons, markers, and stickers.

For a different effect, cover the binoculars with foil or construction paper before decorating. Or tape circles of colored cellophane to the ends of each roll to give the viewer a colorful look at the world.

Then punch a hole at one end on the outside edge of each tube. Tie enough yarn through the holes so that the binoculars slip easily over your child's head. Now go for a walk and look for birds!

Bev Therkelsen
Andover, MA

Deb Olander
Andover, MA

Sylvia Stephenson
Deedee Roberts
Family Cooperative
Preschool
N. Andover, MA

Nancy Laorenza
N. Andover, MA

ANIMAL VISITS

Petting zoos or local farms that cater to the public are great places to spend some time with your child. You may find a large variety of animals there including horses, goats, sheep, pigs, ducks, chickens, and dogs. Bring a bag of carrots as a treat for the animals.

Pat Picard
Andover, MA

PERFECT PICNIC

Look for a botanical garden, arboretum, or conservatory in your area. Often, they are the "best-kept secrets" in your community. The grounds are often filled with magnificent gardens and flowering trees. You'll find it is a perfect spot for a quiet family picnic.

Nancy Maher
Andover, MA

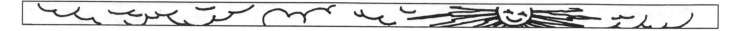

SHOE BOX CONSTELLATIONS

glue	shoe box
paint	paintbrush
ice pick	construction paper

First cut a peephole in one end of an old shoe box. Then have your child paint the inside of the shoe box to resemble the night sky. When the paint has dried, help your child mark her favorite constellation on the inside of one end of the box. Be sure to have a book on constellations handy. Using an ice pick, punch a small hole where each "star" is located. For an added special effect, spray paint the outside of the box black. Then let your child decorate it with paper cutouts of stars and planets. Point the box toward a light source and look through the peephole. The constellation will stand out clearly as the light comes through the holes. After it's dark, try to identify your child's constellation in the night sky.

Mary Pritchard
Andover, MA

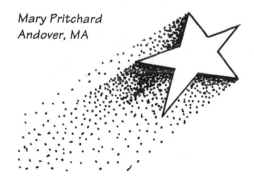

HIGH SCHOOL ATHLETICS

A high school athletic event is entertaining for young children. The games are usually played in the early afternoon, or in the morning during school vacations. The boys' and girls' high caliber of play and full uniforms make them look like professional athletes to young children!

Look for baseball, soccer, field hockey, and softball games. On days when it is too cold or wet to be outside, enjoy a basketball game or a gymnastics meet.

Jane Cairns
Andover, MA

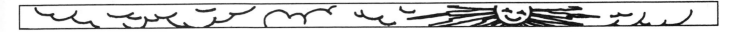

TAKE ME OUT TO THE BALLGAME

bat	fabric markers
stencils	painter's caps
ball	white T-shirts

This activity Involves an art project, a softball or tee ball game, a song, and lunch or a snack.

Begin by dividing a group of children into two teams, such as the Stegosaurus and the Triceratops. Have each child stencil her number and the team symbol onto a T-shirt and hat using fabric markers. An exciting game of softball or tee ball follows. Afterwards, the players may lunch on Fenway franks or snack on peanuts and popcorn while singing "Take Me Out To The Ballgame."

Myrna Schoen
Andover, MA

HIKE INTO FAIRYLAND

Make a walk more interesting by creating an exciting name for your destination. For example, call it Fairyland, Fantasyland, or Monsterland, and elaborate on the story as you go.

We take walks in the woods and call it Fairyland. We find little wrapped candies along the trail (Dad sneakily walks ahead), and we make up stories about why the fairies left the candies on the ground.

Linda Beg
Andover, MA

BOWS AND ARROWS

string	sticks
straws	scissors

Have your child find a long, straight stick and then fashion a bow out of it by tying a piece of string from one end of the stick to the other. You can make arrows by notching some straws on one end. Then let your kids outside to enjoy an afternoon in the wild west.

NOTE: As a safety precaution, cover the unnotched end of each straw with masking tape and be sure to closely supervise your children.

Lisa Buitenhuys
Andover, MA

HULA HOOPS

Hula hoop activities encourage simple fun. Place a series of hoops on the ground and jump or hop in and out of them.

Hold a hoop vertically and encourage your child to creep or walk through it. Hold the hoop horizontally a few inches off the ground and have your child step or jump into it.

Raise the hoop a foot off the ground and encourage her to creep under it and stand up. Then have her hold on to the hoop while you gently shift her weight in all directions.

Andi Larsen
Andover, MA

BEDSHEET PARACHUTE

There are a number of different games you can play with a parachute fashioned out of an old bedsheet. First, sit in a circle with friends or family members and shake the bed sheet, making waves. Then have the children sit on top of the sheet as you make the waves. Stand up and drag the sheet, with the children on it, back and forth across the ground.

Have the children sit or lie on the ground in the middle of the circle while the adults puff the sheet over the children's heads and let it float down. See who can get out from under the sheet before the sheet touches them.

Stand up and let the children get back on the sheet. While holding the edges of the sheet, have the adults walk or run in a circle singing "Ring Around The Rosie."

Andi Larsen
Andover, MA

MILK CARTON BOWLING

markers	construction paper
plastic ball	10 qt.-size milk cartons

Here is an easy way to bring a bowling alley into your backyard. Cover ten milk cartons with construction paper and number them from 1 to 10. Set up the cartons in a bowling pin formation. Have your children take turns rolling a plastic ball toward the cartons. Older children can count the number of cartons that fall and the number that remain standing.

Nancy Maher
Andover, MA

SLEEPING GIANT

The object of this game is to capture the treasure that a "sleeping" giant is guarding.

Pick something, such as a tree, to be home base. Have the person who is playing the giant lie down 25 feet or more away from the tree with the treasure by his side. (The treasure can be any object of your choosing.)

Play starts with the other players gathered at home base. They must figure out a plan to capture the treasure without being tagged by the giant. For example, one person might distract the giant while the others try to capture the treasure.

Once the game begins, the giant is free to stand up and move around. If a player moves off home base and is tagged by the giant, he becomes the giant's prisoner and must remain frozen in place. He can only be unfrozen if another player tags him.

Play continues until the giant captures all the players, or a player grabs the treasure and makes it back to home base.

Meg Dallett
Andover, MA

FLASHLIGHT TAG

This is a game my children and I loved to play when they were younger. On a warm night, I would get a flashlight and tell the kids they had five minutes to hide outside. The object of the game was for me to find and "tag" them with the beam of my flashlight.

Now there is an art to being "it" in Flashlight Tag. When the children were young, I simply walked around outside with the flashlight on pretending not to see them. As the children got older, the game became more sophisticated and we constantly tried to outsmart one another. For example, the kids often climbed trees, hoping I'd forget to look up as I passed by. Sometimes, I'd climb a tree and wait quietly for an unsuspecting victim to creep by below me—then I'd pounce on them with a roar. My children tell me that if I unknowingly passed by their hiding place, they would sneak out and follow me!

It was not long after we started playing this game that I began stalking them with the flashlight turned off. With years of practice, I became adept at walking silently in the dark. Once I outsmarted myself when I heard a rustling under the apple tree. I leapt forward with a roar, turning the flashlight on. Before me stood a deer with a huge rack of antlers, munching an apple. It was hard to tell who was more surprised -- he or I!

John Fletcher
Brentwood, NH

ICE HOUSE

I used to make ice bricks in Minnesota as a child and feel nostalgic whenever I do this activity with my own children.

Fill empty milk cartons with water and freeze them to make ice bricks. Let them thaw slightly before unwrapping them. Your children can use the bricks outside to build a wall or even a house. Use snow to "cement" the bricks together. For a stained glass effect, add food coloring to the water before freezing it.

Elizabeth Rose
Georgetown, MA

RAINBOW SNOWMAN

If your children are enthusiastic snowman sculptors, they will be thrilled to discover how to turn their snowman into a rainbowman.

After your children have made a snowman or other type of snow sculpture, provide them with food coloring. Have them paint the sculpture one drop at a time. (Colored water in squirters works well too.) Your children will enjoy watching new colors appear as the colored sculpture melts and the original colors blend together.

Meredith Johnson
Andover, MA

COLORED ICE CUBE HUNT

water pitcher	food coloring
ice cube trays	buckets

As a boost to winter doldrums, host a colored ice cube hunt. A few weeks before the hunt, make as many trays of colored ice cubes as possible. Mix water and food coloring in a pitcher, stir with a spoon, then pour into ice cube trays. Your children will have a glorious time mixing batches of different colors. Experiment with the first batch of ice cubes to learn how much food coloring you need to add to make brightly colored cubes.

When the big day comes, make sure that each child brings a bucket, but have a few extra on hand just in case. After all the children have arrived, send a parent outside to scatter hundreds of ice cubes around the yard. Hopefully, there will be snow on the ground because the colored ice cubes make a festive sight on snow, but it is fun without snow too.

Once the ice cubes have been scattered, the children can hunt for the cubes. When all the cubes have been found, gather the group for a photo, and encourage them to pile their bounties into one, BIG ice cube mountain. This is an exciting activity to do at a Valentine's Day Party.

NOTE: Tell parents to send mittens that won't be ruined if they become more colorful!

Mary Pritchard
Andover, MA

For great year-round entertainment, fill your plastic pool with materials other than water, such as large pieces of foam, pillows, tennis balls, leaves in the fall, or snow in the winter.

Andi Larsen
Andover, MA

One of our favorite winter activities is going for a walk in the woods after it has snowed. We look for animal tracks and try to identify the animal that made them. Then we follow the tracks until another set of tracks catches our eye.

Jeremy Foy
N. Andover, MA

When bringing the kids to the beach, load the cooler, towels, beach bags, and toys onto a plastic winter sled. You can pull all the equipment along the sand, and still hold the kids' hands during the walk from the car to the beach.

Pat Picard
Andover, MA

Empty cereal boxes are a great way to transport a batch of cupcakes. Simply cut a large flap in the front of the cereal box. Add the cupcakes and close the flap. Your cupcakes are now ready to go to the playground for a special play group snack.

Bev Therkelsen
Andover, MA

When bringing an infant or toddler to the beach, bring a small inflatable pool and fill it with water and toys. It will keep the little ones out of the waves and make it much easier to keep track of them.

Pat Picard
Andover, MA

The next time you take a walk in the woods, bring a bag along for collecting trash.

Bobbie Lantow
Andover, MA

Carry a cooler in your car for storing groceries on hot days. Then if you stop to play at a playground on the way home from the supermarket, you can store your perishables in the cooler.

Bev Therkelsen
Andover, MA

A wildlife sanctuary is a wonderful place for hiking and picnicking. Look in the Yellow Pages—or ask around—for one near your home. It's an all-day activity!

Nancy Sullivan
Andover, MA

Plan a family or neighborhood recital on the lawn. The children can all take turns displaying their talents by dancing, singing, or doing gymnastics and swing set tricks while parents relax on lawn-chairs. Have an intermission and serve refreshments.

Valerie Taylor
Houston, TX

Tired of sand underfoot in your house? Keep a container of baby powder at the back door. The next time you find yourself face-to-face with a sand-covered youngster, simply sprinkle baby powder onto his hands and feet. The sand will brush right off!

Elizabeth Fletcher Foy
N. Andover, MA

Bring water and plaster of Paris to the beach to make sand castings. Make a shallow hole in the sand and let your child line it with treasures she has found on the beach. Pour in the plaster and let it harden for 15 minutes. Dig it up and let it dry for several hours before brushing away the excess sand.

David Tremaine
Spokane, WA

RAINY DAY
ACTIVITIES

GREETING CARD BOX

Find a special box (an old shoe box will do) and save all your greeting, holiday, and birthday cards. On a rainy day, or when you need a quiet activity, bring out the special box and let your child look at or color on the cards. Your child may want to decorate the box as well.

Nancy Laorenza
N. Andover, MA

RAIN PICTURES

Give your child a piece of sturdy paper and let him color on it using paint or markers. When he is done, place his artwork out in the rain and watch the colors run together. On a sunny day, use a squirt bottle to make your own rain.

Cathy Greene
N. Andover, MA

WHAT'S MISSING?

This is a memory game. Lay a few objects on the table and let your child study them for a few minutes. Then tell your child to turn away. While he is not looking, remove something from the table. Then tell your child to turn around and figure out what's missing.

Emily Yukich
Boston, MA

MOVING TO MUSIC

Using classical or modern music, or by tapping out rhythms on objects, have children move to the beat of the music. They can move slowly to the slow beats and quickly to the fast beats. With staccato beats, the children can jump up and down like popcorn or raindrops. With an adagio tempo, they can move more gracefully, like a butterfly.

VARIATION: This Stop and Go Dance Game is a sure crowd pleaser. Turn on the radio or stereo and use the volume control to signal the starting and stopping of the dance. When the music is on, the children dance as fast as they can. When the music is turned off, they must freeze in whatever position they are in. You will probably tire of this game long before your children!

Beth Sauerbrunn
N. Andover, MA

BALLOON TENNIS

Balloons are large enough for preschoolers to hit and less dangerous than balls for indoor play.

Make some tennis rackets by taping paint stirrer sticks to plastic plates. Blow up some helium-quality balloons and then let your children hit the balloons back and forth across the room. Older children can count how many times they can hit it, alone or with a partner, without letting it touch the ground.

<u>VARIATION</u>: My child's occupational therapist showed us how to make plastic bats out of one-liter plastic bottles. First cut the bottoms off two of these bottles. Tape the two bottoms together using duct tape. Hang a balloon from the ceiling. Then use your home-made bat to hit it.

Jill McLaughlin   *Denise Iozzo*
Andover, MA   *Reading, MA*

FLASHLIGHT EXPLORATION

For some spooky fun on a dark winter night, turn off all the lights in the house. Then give each child a flashlight and explore the house together.

Scott Richardson
Andover, MA

PAPER FIGHTS

Cooped up inside with energetic preschoolers or elementary school children? Stage a paper fight to help them let off some steam. Make each child or team a "fort" behind armchairs. Then arm them with balls of rolled up newspaper and let them throw their ammunition at one another. Join in the fun if you feel like it!

Gerry Pouliot
Andover, MA

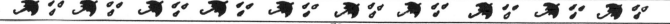

LET'S GO FISHING

string	contact paper
magnets	construction paper
paper clips	wooden spoons or dowels

Using colored construction paper, cut out about 20 fish and cover them with clear contact paper. Place a large paperclip over the nose of each fish and put the fish in a box.

Make a fishing rod by tying a magnetic kitchen hook to a piece of string and then attaching the other end of the string to a dowel, stick, or wooden spoon.

Now let your child fish. Ask her to catch all the blue fish and then all the red fish. Count them. "Cook" them. Then throw them back in and start again.

Jody Brickman
Andover, MA

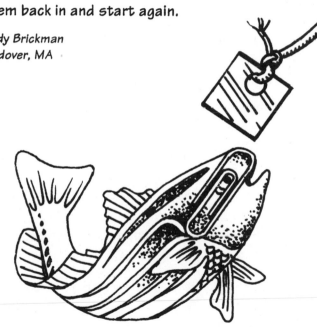

SELF-PORTRAIT

Tell your child she is going to draw a huge picture of herself.

If you have paper on a roll, cut off a piece long enough for your child to lie down on. If not, simply tape large pieces of paper together.

Lay the paper on the floor and trace your child's outline onto the paper. Then let her color in her face and clothes.

Chalk, paint, fabric, buttons, yarn, or any collage material may be used to liven up your child's picture of herself.

Claudia Simon
Andover, MA

PAPER HOUSE

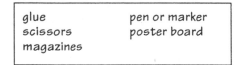

glue	pen or marker
scissors	poster board
magazines	

Draw the outline of a house on a large piece of poster board complete with as many rooms as you like. Then search through magazines with your child to find items with which to furnish and decorate your paper house. When your child finds something she likes, help her cut it out and paste it onto the house. If you use tac-it glue, your child will be able to rearrange her paper house.

VARIATION: Cut out the windows of the house and have your child tape photographs of family members in the windows. Your child's picture could appear in his room and the family's dog could peek out of a dog house in the backyard.

Andrea Lederfine   *Ann Handley*
Andover, MA   *Tewksbury, MA*

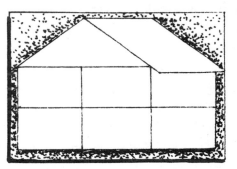

CARDBOARD PLAYHOUSE

paint	markers
scissors	crayons
large box	

Cut out windows on three sides of a large box. Leave the fourth side open or use pre-existing flaps as a doorway for the house. Help your child decorate the house inside and out using markers, crayons, or paint. Draw bricks, clapboards, shingles, shrubs, trees, or flowers on the outside and curtains, toys, animals, bookshelves, or whatever will make the house seem cozy on the inside. Then, let the fun begin.

As a toddler, my son, Daniel, used his house to play peek-a-boo through the windows. Over the past year, it has become a puppet theatre, a secret hiding place, and a fire station in which he houses his favorite fire engines.

Susan Siegel
Daniel Pouliot
Andover, MA

CLUB TICKETS

Using square pieces of paper, have your child write "invitations" to friends to join his club. This is a good activity for children learning to write letters. Your child can then decorate the envelopes and write the invitee's name on each envelope. I use stickers as substitute stamps.

Jay Geary
Andover, MA

POSTCARDS AND MAILBOX

Make a mailbox out of a shoe box by cutting a flap in its lid large enough to accommodate standard size photographs. Have your child decorate the mailbox with crayons or markers. Talk about who you would like to send postcards to and then write the names on the back of leftover double prints of a family outing or vacation. Let your child "stamp" the homemade postcards with stickers or a stamp. Now your postcards are ready to mail in the mailbox!

Deb Olander & Ryan Ferguson
Andover, MA

FOOD PICTURES

| scissors | construction paper |
| coupons | |

Sunday is our son's favorite day of the week. When the Sunday paper arrives, he can be found, scissors in hand, pouring through the coupon sections, looking at pictures of food. What happens next is different each week. One week, he may compile a scrapbook and organize the foods by groups. Another time, he may use the pictures as part of a collage or special project for a friend. Every week I am convinced there is no end to his "food" ideas. Every week I am also convinced there is no end to the scraps of paper in his room. (We're working on that!)

Bobbie Lantow
Andover, MA

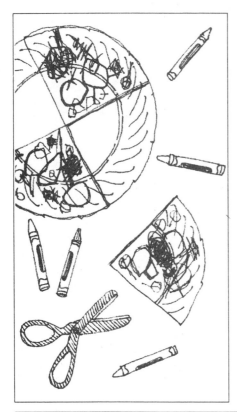

PAPER PIZZAS

crayons   paper plates
scissors

Homemade pizza is a favorite in our house. When we're not preparing one to eat, I often find our son creating "pizzas" with paper plates.

Plain white paper plates work best—he says—and the project requires two of them. One plate becomes a pizza pan and he cuts the second plate into pieces (halves, quarters, or eighths). Each piece is lovingly colored and designed to make a pizza connoisseur smile.

Bobbie Lantow
Andover, MA

REFRIGERATOR MOSAIC

Collect the colored lids from your milk containers for a few weeks. You will be amazed at the colors you acquire, especially if you vary the brand of milk you buy.

Glue magnets on the back of each plastic top. Then let your child create mosaic patterns on the refrigerator.

NOTE: You can purchase magnets as a roll that can be cut to size or as individual pieces at a craft, office supply, or dime store.

Norma Villarreal
Andover, MA

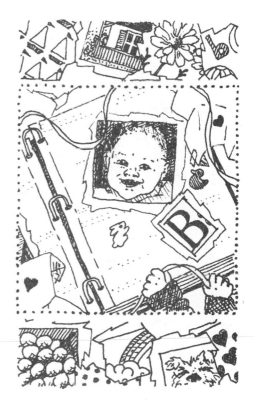

A BOOK ABOUT ME

glue	magazines
markers	construction paper
scissors	

Staple construction paper together to make a book and title it "Me." Next, label the pages with some of the following headings: Parts of the Body, Favorite Foods or Colors, Family Names or Members, My House, My Pet, My Favorite Activities, My Favorite Books. Then let your child create her book. For example, on the page labeled "My Hands," your child might make hand prints. Encourage her to cut out magazine pictures of her favorite foods and glue them on the "My Favorite Foods" page. Paste a picture of the family pet on the "My Pet" page. The creative possibilities are endless.

VARIATION: Pick a theme such as boy's faces, girl's faces, pets, food, toys, or clothes. Look through newspapers or magazines together and find pictures that fit this theme. Let your child cut out the pictures and arrange them on a piece of paper. Then glue them in place.

Emily Newman
Lowell, MA

Susan Bourland
Andover, MA

RAINBOW TOAST

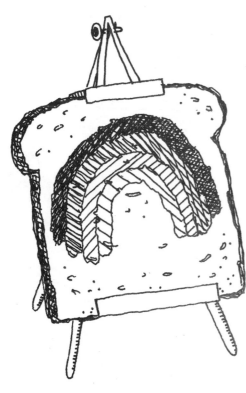

milk	small containers
white bread	clean paintbrushes
food coloring	

My children enjoy creating their own Toasted Art Gallery at the breakfast table.

In a small container, mix a few drops of food coloring with approximately two tablespoons of milk. (The plastic caps from pump toothpastes make great containers!) I usually have red, green, blue and yellow "paint" available in four different containers.

Using a clean paintbrush, let your child paint on a slice of bread. Then toast the bread and let your child admire her toast art!

Anna Duke Reach
Marietta, GA

BREAD PLAY DOUGH

Divide some refrigerated bread dough among your children and let them form the dough into various shapes. We enjoy making pretzels, twists, braids, circles, numbers, and letters. For easier cleanup, let the children work on a cookie sheet. Then bake their creations according to the directions on the package and enjoy!

Bettina Turner
Haverhill, MA

SHAVING CREAM FUN

paper	shaving cream or
cookie sheet	instant pudding

This activity is so simple, yet it is a sure kid pleaser. Spread shaving cream on the kitchen counter. Then let your kids play with it as if it were finger paint. Shaving cream never stains clothing and your counter will be spotless after you wipe off the shaving cream.

If you have very young children let them finger paint with instant pudding. (Shaving cream stings if it gets in the eyes.) Place a piece of paper on a cookie sheet to keep the "paint" from getting all over the table. Cleanup is a cinch—just let your kids lick their fingers clean!

Vicki Iannazzi
Andover, MA

Audrey Price
N. Andover, MA

WATER AND SNOW PLAY

When it's too cold or wet to do water play outside, have water play in the kitchen! Spread an old vinyl tablecloth over the floor. Fill a baby bathtub or dishpan with warm water. Have a variety of toys on hand, including cups, bottles, measuring spoons, and funnels. If you want your children to stay dry, have them wear plastic smocks or let them "dress up" in their raincoats. Then let them sit around the tub and have a splash!

On snowy days when my children just can't stop playing in the snow, I bring the fluffy, white stuff inside. I let them play with it as described earlier. They especially love to watch it melt!

Marcia Strykowski
Bradford, MA

Shelly Selwyn
Andover, MA

Barbara Moverman
N. Andover, MA

COUPON CLIPPING

One Sunday morning while my husband and I were attempting to read the paper, Alex and Sira were pulling apart the coupon circulars pointing to all the things they would like on the next trip to the grocery store. Then it dawned on me that I could keep them busy by enlisting their help in cutting coupons. The kids have so much fun helping out and we save money in the process. I even let the kids choose one thing they can buy for their effort!

Pattye Grant
West Boxford, MA

FAMILY RECORD

glue	ribbon/yarn
glitter	family photos
scissors	colored pencils
markers	construction paper
hole punch	

Cut several sheets of construction paper into 5 by 7 inch pieces. Next, cut some family photographs into a variety of fun shapes. Let your child glue up to three photographs onto each sheet of paper. Leave room on each page to briefly describe what is happening in each picture or group of pictures.

Help your child make a cover for his book by cutting two 5 by 7 inch pieces out of a sheet of cardboard. Then let him decorate the cover with glitter, construction paper, felt, and/or markers.

Punch two holes along one side of the front and back cover and each of the pages in the photo album. Thread some ribbon through the holes to bind the pages into a book and tie securely. This method allows you to expand the book later.

<u>Variation</u>: Cut out just the faces of family members and let your child arrange them on a piece of construction paper. Then glue them in place. It's also fun to use these cutouts to make cards, invitations, and announcements.

Joe & Ryan Ferguson
Andover, MA

Jay Geary
Andover, MA

Linda Francalancia-Hacker
Andover, MA

SEWING FUN

I have an old sewing box that I have filled with empty spools of thread, shoe laces, and assorted pieces of fabric. Whenever I need to sew, Sara takes out her own box and pretends to sew as well. Occasionally, she even tries to thread the spools herself.

Ellen Zuckert
New York, NY

SCHOOL STEPS

In this game, kids advance from preschool to twelfth grade by moving up the steps of a staircase. To begin, have your children sit on the bottom step, which represents preschool. You are the teacher and stand facing your students. Hide a penny in one hand and ask the first child to guess which hand holds the penny. If he chooses correctly, he advances up to the next step and is now in kindergarten. If not, he remains on the same step until his next turn. Play continues until someone reaches the top step and graduates.

Lydia Dallett
Andover, MA

LITTLE CARPENTER AND PAINTER

saw	hammer
tape	screwdriver
nails	paintbrushes
water	cardboard boxes
bucket	

This is a good activity for your child while you are working on a project in the cellar.

Let your child hammer nails or poke holes with a screwdriver into a large cardboard box that has been taped closed. With supervision, let him practice sawing. (It is less frustrating for your child if you make slits in the box beforehand.)

Put some water in a bucket and let your child paint the box with water. He will feel like a real painter and there won't be any mess.

My kids love to be allowed to use real nails and the box provides just enough resistance for them to hammer them in. Plus, the nails are easy to remove.

Melissa Burke
Andover, MA

VEHICLE RAMP AND TUNNEL

| boxes | cardboard |
| glue | masking tape |

This vehicle ramp and tunnel was inspired by the Fisher-Price car garages.

Construct a base for the ramps using a large flat box, like the ones used to package security gates. Fill the box with newspaper to make it sturdy.

Lay this base box flat on the ground. Then glue or tape a tall box to one corner of the flat base box (See illustration.) Glue or tape a second shorter box to another corner of the base.

Connect the two boxes with a ramp. I make my ramps by removing the top and bottom of a small box and cutting off one of its sides. In this way, I form a three-sided piece of cardboard.

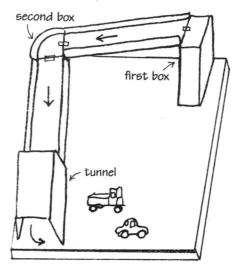

second box

first box

tunnel

Tape your ramp to both boxes and secure its sides with tape to prevent cars from falling off the ramp.

Cut a pie-shaped section out of a Quaker Oats lid and glue it to the top of the second box. The sides of this lid will redirect cars down the next ramp.

Tape a second ramp from the second box down to the flat base box. At the end of this ramp, glue a tunnel in place made out of three sides of a long short box.

My son sits right on the base box to play with his home-fashioned ramp and tunnel set.

Anne Wein
Andover, MA

SCAVENGER HUNT

When we are cooped up inside on a rainy day, we often have a scavenger hunt. I make a list of things I want the children to find. Then I give each child a bag and read off the descriptions one by one, giving them time in between to find an item that meets the description. For example, I might ask them to find something that is blue or hard or fuzzy. An added benefit of this game is that the kids get some exercise running around looking for things and I get to watch them while relaxing on the couch!

Nancy Chandler
N. Andover, MA

ACTIVITIES FROM THE COUCH

On those days when I can't seem to get energized, I rely on my handy repertoire of activites from the couch.

One of my children's favorite games is "The Sleeping Game." I feign sleep while my kids sneak up on me. Every so often, I feebly reach out to grab, and miss, one of them. If I am feeling energetic, I catch and tickle one of them.

Our couch is near a stairway, so we play "Steps." By the count of a large number, say 84, each of my kids is required to find a seat on a step. I must guess, with much fanfare and without looking, which step each child occupies.

"Hide the Button" can be retrofitted for the couch since, with a little practice, I can lob the button into great hiding spots.

Finally, there is "Hide-and-Seek." This is advanced aerobic work, since at some point I must get up and find my children. Remember, check with your doctor before beginning this program.

Loretta Hoffman
Methuen, MA

A timer works wonders to foster sharing among children. When a dispute arises, explain that each child will have five minutes with a toy and then set the timer accordingly. When it dings, the toy is passed to the next child in line.

Bev Therkelsen
Andover, MA

Make a game out of exercising with your child by taking turns being the "leader" and the "follower." Wear leotards to add to the fun. You'll have lots of laughs, get a great workout, and your child will learn the benefit of exercise at a young age!

Wendy Venti
N. Andover, MA

Whenever my children bring home books from the library, I remove the library cards and put them on a high shelf. When it's time to return the books, I count the cards and then know how many books I need to look for on the bookshelf.

Marcia Strykowski
Bradford, MA

Kids love to taste what they've baked. However, they seldom finish a large muffin, so use mini-muffin tins to make kid-size treats.

Julie Lapham
N. Andover, MA

To end the hassle of jumbled and/or misplaced puzzle pieces, flip a puzzle over after completing it. Then write the same preassigned letter, number, or symbol on the back of each puzzle piece. Make sure to place this identical mark on the correct box.

Sharon Hehn
Chelmsford, MA

Let older children put their puzzles together on a cookie sheet. If they don't finish the puzzle in one sitting, it can be easily stored on a shelf until the next session.

Jenny Bixby
Acton, MA

When I want to spend some special time with my two-year-old daughter, we bake cookies together. She enjoys mixing the ingredients, spooning the dough onto the cookie sheet and licking her fingers. Best of all, she gets to eat the end product and tell everyone she baked the cookies.

Linda Blau Traub
Andover, MA

A photo cube is a great way to display emergency phone numbers for children. Put pictures of people or places in the cube and place the number in large print beside the picture. Then leave the cube by the phone.

Marlies Zammuto
Andover, MA

To prevent your child from sitting too close to the T.V., place a masking tape line on the floor to sit behind.

Lynne Doxsey
Andover, MA

If you are coping with a power outage in the evening, take the opportunity to turn lantern or candlelight into hand shadow fun.

Mary Pritchard
Andover, MA

Encourage your child to make a map of her own room. Then use the map for a hide-and-seek game. For example, hide something in her room and then show her where you hid it on the map. Help her find it in the room using the map as a guide.

Molly Lemeris
Croton-on-the-Hudson, NY

SCIENCE AND NATURE: EXPERIMENTS AND DISCOVERY IDEAS

THE BEST NEST

yarn	string
glue	cotton balls
twigs	fabric scraps
grass	oak tag/cardboard
straw	

Discuss some bird facts with your children: For example, all birds have features; most birds fly (some, such as ostriches and penguins do not); birds hatch from eggs; they have beaks but no teeth; and most birds build nests. If possible, show your children a real bird's nest. Then have them try to build their own nest.

Provide your children with a variety of nest-building materials, including glue and cardboard or oak tag. Your children can even create their own bird to place in their nest!

NOTE: Birds usually build new nests every year, so you may collect any abandoned nests you find. Using gloves, remove the nest and place it in a plastic bag with a few mothballs. Leave it for a few days to take care of any insects that were living in the nest. Then let your child hold and examine the nest.

Nancy Maher
Andover, MA

DRUMLIN FARM BIRD FEEDER

string	1 c. hot water
large bowl	2 c. oatmeal
1 c. flour	1 lb. lard, melted
4 c. birdseed	1 grapefruit or orange

Birds will love this winter treat almost as much as your child will enjoy making it.

Combine the oatmeal, birdseed, and flour in a large bowl. Add one cup of hot water. Let your child stir the mixture until all the ingredients are moistened. Then YOU add the melted lard to bind the mixture. Once the mixture is cool enough to handle, let your child knead the combined ingredients thoroughly.

Next, punch three evenly spaced holes around the top edge of an empty grapefruit or orange half. Your child can now spoon the "bird pudding" into the empty fruit half. Let the pudding harden and then tie string through the holes and hang the filled feeder outside.

Add whatever ingredients you have on hand, such as breadcrumbs, dried fruit, and scraps of meat. Simply use 1/2 pound of fat for every pound of filler.

Sharon Hehn
Chelmsford, MA

PINE CONE BIRD FEEDER

string	birdseed
pine cones	peanut butter

Children will enjoy making these pine cone bird feeders. First, have your child cover a pine cone with peanut butter. Then roll the peanut butter-covered pine cone in birdseed. Tie a string to its top end and your feeder is ready to hang outside.

Sharon Hehn
Chelmsford, MA

NESTING SACK

Providing birds with nesting materials is a satisfying activity for young bird enthusiasts. Begin collecting nest building materials such as bits of yarn, dog hair, and dryer lint early in the spring. Have your child stuff the nesting materials into a netted onion sack. Then have her pull tantalizing bits of yarn and lint through the netting to attract the birds. Together, hang the sack in a bush or on the branch of a tree.

In April, we hung our sack on our lilac bush. We were soon rewarded by a flurry of activity around the sack. Our most frequent shoppers were a pair of tufted titmice who spent several days pulling out fluff and flying to their woodland nest-in-progress.

Emily and David Tremaine
Spokane, WA

WHAT'S IN MY BAG?

This activity is a great way to introduce children to "seeing" with their hands. It also provides them with a perspective of the visually challenged.

Blindfold your child and have him put his hand into a paper bag filled with a variety of small household objects. After your child has selected an object, ask him to identify it using his hands to feel its shape and dimension.

Then let your child have a turn filling the bag and watching you guess what's inside.

Vivian Dowsett
N. Andover, MA

SOUND EFFECTS

Encourage your child to develop her ear for sounds by recording different noises. Using a tape recorder, make recordings when you go to the zoo, into the city, or even out into your backyard. Make recordings of different activities you do at home, such as brushing your teeth, washing the dishes, or turning the pages of a book. It's fun to listen to the recordings together and try to identify the sounds. You might also try to incorporate the sound effects into a story or puppet show.

Elizabeth Fletcher Foy
N. Andover, MA

SCENT-SATIONAL DISCOVERIES

Poke holes in the lids of some clean, empty yogurt containers. Put a different scented candle in each container and cover them with their lids. On the bottom of each container, make a note of the type of scent in the container. Let your child smell the containers and try to identify each scent.

<u>Note:</u> Cotton balls soaked in peppermint, orange, and almond extracts are another medium for scent games.

Marlies Zammuto
Andover, MA

UNDERWATER SCOPE

duct tape	clean milk carton
plastic wrap	

Cut the top and bottom off a paper milk carton. Secure a piece of plastic wrap over one end of the carton using waterproof duct tape. Seal the sides well to prevent leakage. Now your child is ready to see underwater! Simply hold the scope, plastic wrap side down, in the water and let your child explore.

Valarie Giarrusso
N. Andover, MA

BOLTS AND MAGNETS

I recently gave my son one of my husband's containers of nuts and bolts and a few magnets. He enjoyed threading the nuts and bolts and attracting them with the magnets.

<u>Variation:</u> Larger and more powerful magnets will allow children to "build" on top of them with smaller metal objects.

Pat Picard
Andover, MA

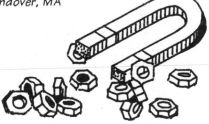

POTATO PRINTS

paint	paper
potatoes	shallow pan

Cut a potato in half and carve a simple shape on the exposed surface. The raised shape should be approximately 1/8 inch to 1/4 inch above the rest of the potato. Have your child dip this printing block in a shallow pan of paint and then stamp with it on a large sheet of paper. Only the raised parts of the block will print.

Shelley Selwyn
Andover, MA

FISH PRINTING

paper	paintbrush
roller	acrylic paints
paper towels	fresh flounder

This is an ancient Japanese art form that is particularly fascinating to children. You may find that your children are as interested in feeling the texture of the fish as they are in making the print.

Lay a whole, uncut fish on a flat surface and have your child paint one side of the fish. Make sure the paint is spread evenly over the fish. Place a piece of paper over the painted fish and use a roller to press the paper onto the fish. Peel the paper off the fish and enjoy the print.

You may find that you need to thin the paint with water to produce a clearer print. To change colors, simply wipe the old paint off the fish with a paper towel.

VARIATION: This same technique can be used with a number of different fruits and vegetables. An apple, cut in half, makes a lovely print, as does a large leaf.

Kate Anderson
Community Cooperative
Nursery School
N. Andover, MA

MAGIC WRITING

Have your child draw a picture using lemon juice as "paint" and a Q-tip as a "paintbrush." After her picture dries, YOU iron over it using low heat. Your child's picture will appear like magic!

VARIATION: Have your child draw a picture using an unlit wax candle. Then let her paint her picture with watercolors. Her invisible picture will appear because the watercolor will adhere to the paper, but not to the wax.

Audrey Price
N. Andover, MA

COLOR MAGIC

wax paper	pencil
crayons	paper

Give your child some crayons and a sheet of wax paper and have her color on one side of the wax paper with a variety of colors. Place a blank piece of paper on the table and put the wax paper on top of it, colored side down.

Using a pencil, have your child make a line drawing on the back of the wax paper. Like magic, her picture will transfer to the paper in multiple colors. Be sure to have your child press hard with both the crayons and the pencil.

VARIATION: Cover a piece of white poster board with different colors of wax crayons. Then color over these multicolored layers with a black crayon. Your child can now scratch patterns through the black to the colorful layers below using her fingernail.

Shelley Selwyn
Andover, MA

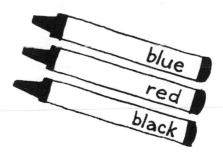

blue
red
black

FROM CATERPILLAR TO MOTH

gypsy moth caterpillars	bug jar leaves for food

My daughter, Sarah, initiated this experiment when she brought home three gypsy moth caterpillars. We put them in a large bug jar equipped with breathing holes and fed them small branches of leaves from the tree on which she had found them.

Every night the caterpillars would consume the leaves we had fed them the day before. Every day we replenished their supply. As they grew, we noticed they shed their skins. We fed them for several weeks. One morning, we looked into the jar and couldn't find them. However, Sarah quickly noticed a cocoon hidden among the

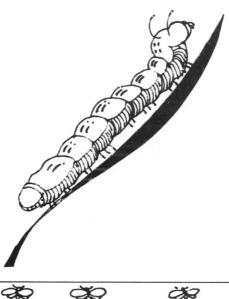

leaves. We checked the jar every day. About a week later, we looked in the jar and were startled to see a white moth fluttering around. It was really magical!

Then an interesting thing happened. When Sarah took the jar outside, a flurry of moths descended upon her. She put the jar down and backed away. The cloud of moths continued to flutter around the jar. Apparently, Sarah's moth was a female sending out pheromones and we had an impromtu lesson on the mating habits of gypsy moths.

Elizabeth Fletcher Foy
N. Andover, MA

CONTAINER GARDENING

seeds	potting soil
water	plastic milk containers

You can start an indoor flower or vegetable garden at any time of the year. However, if you are planning to transplant the seedlings outside, the instructions on the back of the packet will help you determine when to start them.

Cut the top off a milk carton, leaving the handle attached. Using a nail, punch drainage holes in the carton. Next, dampen the soil and put it in the container. Bury the seeds to the depth specified on the seed packet. Then put the container in a plastic bag and store it in a warm, dark place. Check the container daily.

When the seeds have sprouted, remove the container from the plastic bag and place the planter on a plate or tray in a sunny spot. Keep the soil moist, but not soggy. Thin the seedlings as directed on the seed packet, fertilize them, and watch them grow!

<u>VARIATION:</u> Draw a face on a paper cup and glue ears to either side of the cup. Then fill the cup with soil and plant some grass seeds in it. Keep the soil moist. As the seedlings grow, your child can enjoy clipping his paper cup person's "hair!"

Sandra McMath
Haverhill, MA

Lucia Carelli
Methuen, MA

PAPER PLATE SNAKES

paper plates	crayons
scissors	black marker

Visit the children's room at your library and select some fictional and nonfictional books about snakes. (One of our favorite snake stories is The Day Jimmy's Boa Ate The Wash.) After reading the story to your child, talk about snakes and look at pictures of different snakes. Then have your child make her own snake by drawing a spiral line on a paper plate. (See illustration.) Let your child color the plate to resemble a real or imaginary snake. Draw an eye at the center of the spiral. Then cut along the black line and a snake will uncoil before your child's eyes!

Kathy DiMura
Methuen, MA

ROCK MANIA

pen	newspaper
tape	shoe box lid
hand lens	plastic bags
notebook	Rock & Mineral Guide
back pack	

Encourage your child to start a rock collection by organizing a family rock hunt. Mark each specimen found on your expedition with a piece of masking tape and an identification number. Help your child record each identification number in her notebook and write down where and when the specimen was found. Have your child place each specimen in a small plastic bag and store them in her back pack. Crumbly rocks can be wrapped in newspaper. Once home, help your child identify each of the rocks in her collection using a Rock and Mineral Guide. Then let her examine each specimen more closely using a hand lens. Your child can display her collection by gluing the labeled rocks onto the lid of a shoe box.

Sue Siegel
Andover, MA

HOMEMADE RAINBOWS

My two-and-a-half-year-old discovered that a glass of water on a sunny windowsill casts a rainbow on the floor. To make the colors more pronounced, we put a sheet of white paper on the floor. Then we used crayons to trace their shape.

An older child might be inspired to learn about prisms: explain that the light going into the glass is bent twice, once when it enters and once when it leaves, causing the light to separate into its component colors.

Jane Cairns
Andover, MA

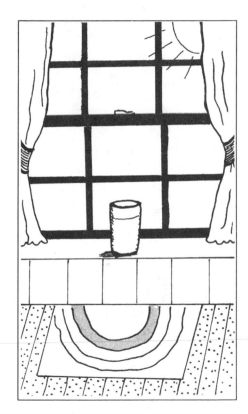

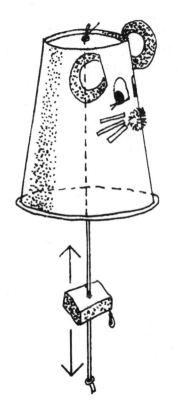

BARKING BELL

glue	15 in. string
ice pick	large plastic cup
markers	construction paper
sponge	

Have your child decorate a large plastic cup using markers and construction paper to make it look like her favorite animal. Poke a small hole in the center of the base of the cup. Thread the string through the hole. Then knot and tape the string to the outside base of the cup to hold it securely in place. Holding the cup upside down, cut the string so that it extends approximately 6 to 8 inches beyond the rim of the cup. (See diagram.)

Using an ice pick, poke a hole in the center of a piece of sponge. Thread the sponge onto the string. Then wet the sponge and push it all the way up the string until it touches the inside bottom of the cup. Hold the cup upside down so that it resembles a bell. Have your child reach her hand up into the cup, squeeze the sponge, and pull it down the string. She will be surprised by a barking sound. Experiment with different sized cups and thicknesses of string to create a variety of sounds.

Denise Iozzo
Reading, MA

NATURE CASTS

Using play dough, your child can make casts that reveal the rich variety of textures that exist in nature.

Press a ball of play dough or clay against the bark of a tree to record its surface texture. Make casts of the bark of different trees in your backyard and compare them.

You can make casts of any textured surface, including bricks and concrete.

Susan Siegel
Chicago, IL

NATURE WALK

To get couch potatoes outside, invite them on a nature walk. Give each child a basket and have her scout for treasures. Typical treasures include rocks, leaves, and pine cones. You can also scout for treasures in your backyard. After returning from your walk, give the children some chalk and let them trace the outline of the treasures they just found. A sidewalk, driveway, patio, or even the garage floor is a great place for this activity.

Eadie Schatz   *Susan Richardson*
W. Hartford, CT   *Andover, MA*

LEAF COLLECTING

iron	collector's notebook
wax paper	freshly picked leaves

My grandchildren, now all grown up, tell me this was an activity they looked forward to whenever they came to visit me.

I would take them on a nature walk and we would collect leaves from a variety of trees. I'd tell my grandchildren the names of the trees as they collected their leaves. When we got back home, we'd place each leaf between two sheets of wax paper and then I'd run a warm iron over the wax paper. The heat of the iron would seal the wax paper around the leaf and prevent it from drying out.

Each child would then add these new leaves to her collector's notebook, which can be homemade or store-bought, by stapling or taping them in. Lastly, we would write the name of the leaf below each new addition.

Mary H. Kelly
Martha's Vineyard, MA

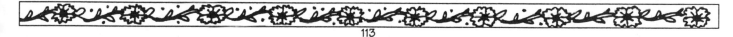

PRESSED FLOWERS

flowers	collector's notebook
contact paper	heavy book/plant press

I still have some of the flowers I pressed with my mother as a child some eighty odd years ago.

After collecting a variety of flowers, simply have your child place each flower between the pages of a very heavy book (use protective paper so that you don't soil the pages) or in a plant press. Leave them undisturbed for two to four weeks.

Once they have dried, remove them and add them to your child's collector's notebook. Be sure to write the name of each flower in the notebook. Pressed flowers can also be preserved by placing them between two sheets of contact paper.

Mary H. Kelly
Martha's Vineyard, MA

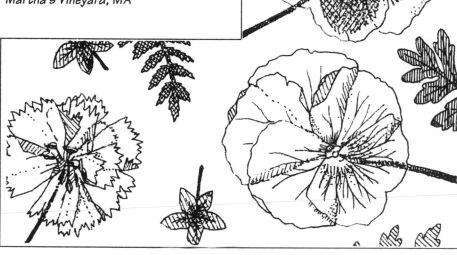

BALL DROP

bell	paintbrush
ball	masking tape
paint	toilet paper rolls
large box	paper towel rolls

This is a quick and easy version of a ball maze at the Acton Discovery Museum in Massachusetts.

PREPARATION

Cut the top flaps off of a large cardboard box and lay the box on its side. Cut some paper towel rolls lengthwise to use as ramps. Cut a hole the size of a toilet paper roll circumference in the top edge of the box, towards the back. You are now ready to construct your maze.

CONSTRUCTION

Stick a toilet paper roll vertically down through the hole in the top of the box and tape it to the back of the box to hold it in place. Tape a paper towel roll, cut lengthwise, to the base of the toilet paper roll and secure it to the back of the box. Be sure to slope the paper towel roll so that the ball will roll. Also, leave enough room at the base of the toilet paper roll for

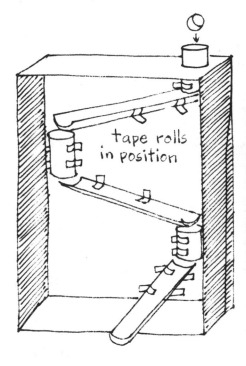

tape rolls in position

the ball to drop through. Place another toilet paper roll, vertically, at the bottom of the paper towel roll and secure it with tape to the back of the box. Continue to alternate toilet paper rolls and paper towel rolls, cut lengthwise, until you reach the bottom of the box. Attach bell at bottom of last tube. The larger the box, the larger and more intricate you can make the maze.

Your children can paint their maze if they wish. Then give them a ball and let them enjoy the show.

Anne Wein
Andover, MA

KITCHEN SINK EXPERIMENTS

bowl	measuring spoons
eye dropper	mixing ingredients
ice cube tray	

We do impromptu kitchen sink experiments by putting a bowl in the kitchen sink and then adding and mixing in all sorts of ingredients. The kids love to see what happens when different reagents are mixed together.

Our favorite reagents include: baking soda, ginger ale (bubbly things are great!), dishwashing liquid, salt, pepper, old spices, and whatever else we may have on hand.

VARIATION 1: Mix vinegar with bicarbonate of soda in a bowl. A huge pile of bubbles will form, much to your children's delight.

VARIATION 2: Fill an ice cube tray with water and add drops of food coloring to four of the cubes. Using the eye dropper, it is then the child's "job" to transfer and mix colors by adding drops of colored water to the clear water.

Susan Ickes
Andover, MA

Nancy Cahan-Landy
Andover, MA

Patti Meade
Andover, MA

COIN POP

Place a small glass bottle in the freezer for five minutes. Then spread petroleum jelly around its rim and cover it with a coin. Let your child warm the bottle by holding it in his hands. Suddenly, the coin will pop off the rim.

As the air in the bottle heats up, it expands, but it is prevented from escaping by the petroleum jelly between the rim and the coin. The pressure continues to build until it is great enough to pop the coin off the rim, letting the air escape.

Robert Reed
Chicago, IL

UNDERWATER VOLCANO

Fill a small bottle with hot water and add <u>ink</u> to it. Tie string around the bottle and lower it into a larger jar filled with cold water. The colored water will rise out of the smaller bottle to the surface of the water like a volcano.

The hot colored water is lighter and more buoyant than the cold water and so it rises to the surface. Once the temperatures of the warm and cold water equalize, the color becomes evenly distributed throughout the jar.

Elizabeth Fletcher Foy
N. Andover, MA

STATIC ELECTRICITY

Mix some salt and ground pepper together on the kitchen counter. Ask your child to separate the salt from the pepper with a plastic spoon. Impossible? Now have her rub the plastic spoon with a woolen cloth. Then hold the spoon above the salt and pepper mixture and slowly lower it. The pepper will jump up to the spoon and remain sticking to it. If your child continues to lower the spoon, the salt will eventually jump up too. The pepper is attracted to the electrically charged plastic spoon first because it is lighter than salt.

Elizabeth Fletcher Foy
N. Andover, MA

OOBLECK

water	plastic cups
bowls	large containers
spoons	plastic tablecloth
cornstarch	

This activity, as easy as it is fun, was inspired by the Dr. Seuss book, <u>Bartholomew and the Oobleck.</u> Lay out a plastic tablecloth on the floor, or have children sit outside at a picnic table or on the grass so clean up will be easy.

Mix two parts cornstarch to one part water. Then let the experimenting begin. Your children will discover that the watery mixture, when squeezed, becomes a solid. However, when held, it melts to its liquid form. Children love to see how oobleck changes back and forth from a liquid to a semi-solid state.

Karen Lawson   *Carla Pond*
Lawrence, MA   *Milford, CT*

HELPFUL HINTS

We have found that paper airplanes made from construction paper fly very well. Let your child decorate them with stickers or crayons. (<u>Note:</u> Use an 8 1/2 by 11 inch piece of paper and make sure all creases are even and straight and that the wings are the same size.)

Lynn Lynch
N. Reading, MA

Gourds make good birdhouses. Wash a fully grown gourd with soap and water and let it dry for a month. Then wax, shellac, or paint the outside. Cut a 1/2 inch hole six inches from the base of the gourd and hang it in a tree.

Sarah Wong
Brookline, NY

Plant a little sapling on your child's birthday and watch the tree grow with your child. Your child will feel proud about having his own special tree and you can explain why his tree is also important to the Earth: it reduces carbon dioxide in the air, provides beauty and shade and is home to many different creatures.

Paula Movsesian
Andover, MA

Encourage your child to keep a journal of the birds she sees in the backyard. Use Roger Tory Peterson's *A Field Guide to Birds* to help identify the birds. Reserve a page in the journal for each bird she sees and let her write down something about the bird or draw its picture.

Lynn McCoy
Reading, MA

A battery charger makes a great gift for new parents and is a smart investment for any family during the years of peak battery usage. Reusable batteries are more expensive than disposables, but they quickly pay for themselves and the charger in both money and convenience. Baby swings, toys, and games are more fun when fresh batteries are always on hand.

Jane Cairns
Andover, MA

Try composting with worms. Build a wooden box, two feet wide by two feet long by eight inches deep. Fill the box with peat moss and add some red worms (available at a local nursery or bait shop). Mix in any household garbage, <u>except</u> meat, bones, or fatty foods. Worms will eat the garbage and make soil.

Susan Siegel
Chicago, IL

Have your child decorate large canvas bags with fabric markers. Then wrap them and give them as gifts. The recipient can use them for grocery shopping and save trees in the process.

Bev Therkelsen
Andover, MA

Consider joining the environmental club, Kids for Saving the Earth. You will receive a monthly newsletter and booklets, stickers, and posters throughout the year. Your child can also submit her own pictures and articles to the newsletter:
  Kids For Saving The Earth
  P.O. Box 47247
  Plymouth, MN 55447-0247

Andrea Margida
Apex, NC

Subscribe to the kids environmental magazine, P-3 (for Planet-3, because Earth is the third planet from the sun). It's a creative and educational magazine:
  P-3, P.O. Box 52
  Montgomery, VT 05470

Martin Wong
Brookline, NY

The disposable mini-muffin trays used by supermarkets are handy for displaying rock collections. Put some cotton in each cup and then lay a rock on each bed of cotton. Use a sticker to label each rock with an identification number. Cover the tray with the clear plastic cover and put another sticker with the rock's name and number above each cup.

Sue Siegel
Andover, MA

SIMPLE TOYS AND GAMES FOR BABY AND TODDLER

HOMEMADE MOBILES

string	colored paper
cardboard	bright fabric
colored felt	

Homemade mobiles are fun and easy to make. Staple a two inch strip of cardboard into a cylinder shape. Poke four evenly spaced holes at the top of the cylinder. Thread string through the holes and make a handle by tying the four pieces of string together above the center of the cylinder.

Next, tie string of various lengths through holes made near the base of the cylinder.

Hang simple, brightly colored objects from these pieces of string. For example, cut shapes from felt or trace objects and animals from board books. Change the objects frequently to renew your infant's interest In her mobile.

Dawn Evans
Sunderland, MA

HOMEMADE CRADLE GYM

Stretch a piece of elastic across the top of your child's crib. Then tie objects of various colors and textures securely to it, such as bold-patterned material, yogurt cartons, plastic toys, and wooden spoons. Change the objects dangling from the gym frequently to give your infant new things to look at, bat at, and admire.

<u>NOTE:</u> As soon as your child can roll over, remove the cradle gym from the crib.

Alice Blaine Jaffe
Andover, MA

BABY POSTER

Many babies like to wake up slowly in the morning. An interesting poster can be just the thing to amuse them.

Cut out pictures of popular cartoon characters, busy babies, or colorful designs. Make a collage of your pictures by gluing them onto a piece of poster board. Hang the poster on the ceiling or wall next to your baby's crib, but out of her reach.

Occasionally glue new pictures over the old ones to renew your child's interest in her poster. As your child grows, she may want to select and paste her own new pictures on the collage.

Marcia Strykowski
Bradford, MA

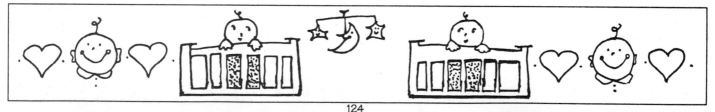

COLIC CURE

We tried everything to soothe our son, Kristopher, during his first colicky months. Finally we hit upon a sure thing. Every night, we would lug out the vacuum cleaner and turn it on. Within minutes, Kristopher would fall asleep. We soon tired of carting the vacuum cleaner around so my husband, David, decided to make a recording of its sound. It worked! For infants who prefer dishwasher, washing machine, or car engine noise, simply tailor the tape to their needs.

Gillian Breckman
Winnipeg, Canada

ACTIVITY CARDS

| glue | art supplies |
| magazines | family photos |

Inspired by the Touch and Feel books, I decided to make my son a collection of personalized activity cards. I pasted family photographs and pictures of some of his favorite things on large pieces of poster board or cardboard. Then I attached various objects of interest to the different cards.

For example, I stapled a cloth over a baby picture for peek-a-boo play. I sewed buttons of different sizes and colors onto a picture of Mickey Mouse. I found a photograph of a car and cut around its doors so they could be opened and closed. Then I pasted the car onto a card and glued a family photo behind each door. This card was my son's favorite.

Anne Wein
Andover, MA

BABY IN A BOX

Find a box large enough for a crawling infant or toddler to sit in. My nine-month-old climbs in and out of boxes with sides that are approximately eight inches high.

Make the box attractive by putting favorite toys, blankets, or plastic containers inside. My daughter often plays happily in her "new place" for a quarter of an hour!

Maureen Denison
Andover, MA

ROLL AND SHAKE BOTTLE

water	1 plastic bottle
liquid soap	food coloring

Our eight-month-old was enthralled by this bottle and our four-year-old liked it so much he snatched it away from his sister.

Fill a one-liter plastic bottle one-third full of water. Add a few drops of liquid soap and food coloring. Close the bottle tightly and let the baby shake or roll it to make bubbles.

David Turner
Haverhill, MA

SPOOL STACKING

Place your spools of thread within your infant's reach and let the games begin! Together stack the spools as high as possible or arrange them into different shapes. Place several spools in covered containers to make musical instruments. Leave the containers uncovered and let your infant drop them into the containers and then dump them out again. Try placing several containers in a row and let your infant transfer the spools from one container to another.

Debbie Ginsberg
Andover, MA

MY DRAWER

Babies as young as eight months love to fill and empty containers. Our children have their own special drawer in the kitchen. We fill it with all kinds of safe and interesting objects such as wooden spoons, pots with tops, large wooden pegs, colorful fabric, and tea strainers. We rotate the objects so there is always something new for them to discover.

An added benefit of this drawer is that I am often able to prepare meals without an infant or toddler on my hip!

Anne Singleton
Wellesley, MA

MORNING SURPRISES

After my daughter, Olivia, goes to sleep at night, we put some soft toys at the bottom of her crib so she'll have something to play with when she wakes up in the morning and -- I admit it-- so my husband and I will get a little extra sleep. (We always keep her crib toys separate from the ones she plays with during the day.)

You can adapt this nightly ritual to an older child by setting up a different scene for her to play with when she wakes up. For example, you might lay a piece of cardboard against the bookshelf with some cars ready to zoom down, or you might set up a tea party on the floor with leftover party hats, plastic cups and saucers, and some stuffed animals as guests. Let your imagination go!

Elizabeth Fletcher Foy
N. Andover, MA

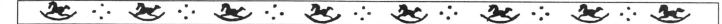

HOMEMADE BLOCKS

Paper bag blocks and milk carton blocks are lightweight and easy for toddlers to lift and stack and they are both easy to make.

PAPER BAG BLOCKS

Fill a paper grocery bag with crumpled up newspaper. Use enough newspaper to make the bag fairly solid. Then slide it inside another empty paper bag to make a large block. (Use paper lunch bags to make smaller blocks.)

Older children may want to use several blocks to build a town, a zoo, or a train. Encourage them to use crayons or markers to decorate the blocks according to the theme of their pretend play.

MILK CARTON BLOCKS

Completely open the top of an empty milk carton. Then cut flaps along the top edge, fold them over, and tape them closed. Cover the cartons with brown paper or contact paper, which is available in a brick design.

Make a collection of these blocks. It is a great way to recycle milk cartons and paper bags!

Marlies Zammuto
Andover, MA

Jody Brickman
Andover, MA

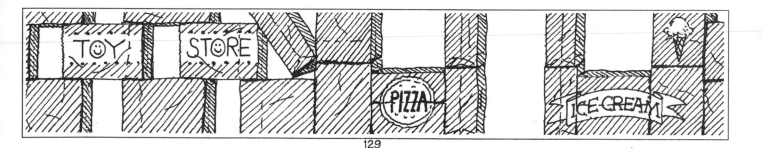

EGG CARTON COLOR SORTER

cardboard	paint
egg carton	12 peg clothespins

It is easy to turn an egg carton into a sorter that helps toddlers recognize different colors. Turn an egg carton upside down. Paint six of the holders and six wooden peg clothespins one color, such as blue, and the other six holders and clothespins another color, such as yellow. When the paint has dried, make a hole in the top of each holder that is large enough to accommodate a peg clothespin.

Give your child the clothespins and ask her to put the yellow clothespins in the yellow holders and the blue clothespins in the blue holders.

Jody Brickman
Andover, MA

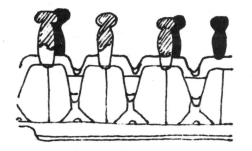

COLOR DAYS

My toddler and I made up this game when he became interested in colors. Once a week, we declare it "Color Day" and Danny gets to choose a color. Throughout the day, we focus on that color as much as possible.

For example, on "Red Day" we dressed in red and enjoyed the attention we got from others who thought we looked silly. After breakfast, which included strawberries and cranberry juice, we collected and played with all the red toys we could find. Before his nap, Danny chose a book about Elmo, a red muppet from Sesame

Street. We counted red cars as we drove through town and had red licorice for a snack. As Danny chose his red pajamas after a dinner of spaghetti and tomato sauce, I was sure that red would not be a color soon forgotten!

Lisa Solomon
Andover, MA

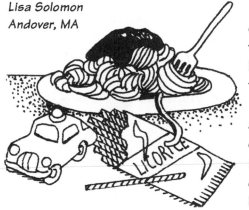

INDOOR SANDBOX

scoops	funnel
bottles	small toys
container	big spoons
puffed rice	dried beans
plastic	coffee beans
tablecloth	

Fill a 13 by 19 inch plastic container with puffed rice, coffee beans, or a variety of dried beans and place it on a plastic tablecloth.

Collect a variety of sifting and pouring toys and let your child shake, scoop, and pour the rice or beans from one container to another. It is also fun to hide small toys under the rice and watch your child discover hidden treasures.

<u>Note:</u> If you have small children who are still mouthing things, use puffed rice rather than beans in the sandbox. As always, be sure to closely supervise small children.

Cathy Greene *Jody Brickman*
N. Andover, MA *Andover, MA*

Maureen O'Dowd *Marlies Zammuto*
Methuen, MA *Andover, MA*

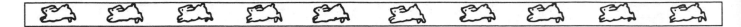

PAPER COLLAGE

| glue | old magazines |
| scissors | construction paper |

An older toddler who can cut with a pair of child-safe scissors will enjoy making this more sophisticated collage. Look through old magazines together and have your child cut out his favorite pictures. My eighteen-month-old loves to cut out pictures of dogs and Mickey Mouse and then arrange and glue them onto construction paper. Once the glue has dried, we color around the pictures.

VARIATION: To encourage shape and color recognition, cut shapes of different sizes and colors out of construction paper. Then let your child use these shapes to make a collage on another piece of construction paper.

Kathy Whelan   *Michele Maldari*
Methuen, MA   *Andover, MA*

NATURE COLLAGE

glitter	cookie sheet
feathers	contact paper
duct tape	nature objects
hole punch	construction paper

Even a young toddler will be successful creating this collage! Place a piece of clear contact paper, sticky side up, on a cookie sheet and tape it down with duct tape. (Using a cookie sheet will prevent things from rolling off the table and will give toddlers in a play group their own space.)

Let your child arrange his treasures, collected on a nature walk, on the contact paper. He can fill in any spaces with glitter, feathers, or different colored holes punched from construction paper. Hang his finished collage in the window.

Marlies Zammuto
Andover, MA

SPICE COLLAGE

glue	construction paper
spices	

Put some glue drops on a piece of construction paper. Then let your toddler sprinkle a different spice on each drop, or let her experiment by sprinkling several different spices on one drop. Once her collage has dried, ask her to smell her artwork and identify the smells she likes best.

Marlies Zammuto
Andover, MA

FINGER PUPPETS

Puppets can really change a mood. For instance, one day when my son was just two, I developed a stable of ready-made puppets. I discovered that just the fingers of one hand could come "alive" to him by merely giving them names and personalities.

For instance, one finger held up was "One," two fingers held up were "Two," and so on. One is very brave, Two is very stubborn, but has good ideas, Three always likes to have a good time and talks in a VERY LOUD VOICE. Four is kind of cautious and fearful and Five likes to sing. I bring out the puppet that best fits the situation.

My son developed a great love for Three when he was turning three and frequently would ask for him while traveling or waiting. He tells Three lots of things he doesn't tell me.

When I need an exit line, I might say, "I've got to go now, I have to help your mom drive the car (or make the lunch, or water the plants)."

Elizabeth Rose
Georgetown, MA

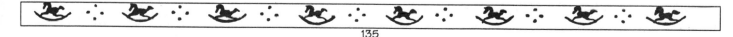

TODDLER PHOTO ALBUMS

Vinyl baseball card protectors (available at card stores for less than a dollar) make great "photo albums" for toddlers. Put some pictures in an order that tells a story about your child's favorite people. As your child gets older, he can arrange the sequence of photos and tell his own stories.

Dick Dietzel
Andover, MA

ICE CUBE ART

My daughter painted with ice cubes at her day care center when she was eleven months old and she loved it.

Have your child dip an ice cube into a small dish of paint and then spread it around on a piece of paper. Your child can re-dip the ice cube into other colors to make a multicolored design.

Joyce Hager
N. Andover, MA

SOCK SORT GAME

Folding laundry seems to be my three-year-old's favorite chore. On numerous occasions, I have folded clothes and placed them in the laundry basket only to turn around and find the clothes "refolded" on the floor or covering the family dog.

However, when I hit upon the idea of putting him in charge of one aspect of the chore, in this case sorting socks, he became a real help. He loves sorting sizes, colors, and patterns.

We end the project with a laundry parade up the stairs with the basket in tow, and he gets to put away his own clothes. Of course a job well done deserves a special snack of popcorn and juice.

Martha Sperandio
Andover, MA

VISUAL ASSOCIATION GAME

My son, Zachary, enjoys making visual associations between the real world and his picture books. Together we have made up a game that reinforces visual connections and builds vocabulary. When he learns a new word we invariably head to his bookshelf. For instance, if my son spotted a dog on an outing, we would look for pictures of dogs. Last summer, after I had planted some pansies, he found a picture of them in one of his books, even though they were a different color from the ones in our garden!

Susan Frish
Andover, MA

GUMDROP TREE

Using some clay as a base, fashion a small tree from a leafless branch. Keep the tree in a special place, bringing it out just before naptime. When your child awakes, one or two gumdrops will have "grown" on the branches of the tree. Small toys, love notes, or stickers can be just as magical.

Doris Patriarca
Tewksbury, MA

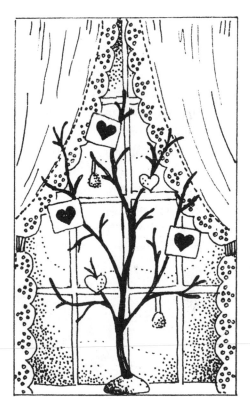

A SONG ABOUT ME

Storytelling by singing songs about aspects of your child's life or special interests can be a powerful way of communicating with your children:

VARIATION 1: When your child is dressed in her pajamas and sitting on her bed, try singing a song about the day's events. Any tune will do. The song can be very detailed or very brief, as time allows. After months of singing to my own child, she has begun making up her own songs to share with me!

VARIATION 2: This activity evolved from my son's request for me to sing a song about one of his favorite storybook characters. I always start with the same first line:

"_____ is a very nice_____"

The song progresses into whatever is happening in my son's life at that point. The songs also help him to work through events that may be making him feel anxious. He always seems relieved if his song friends are experiencing similar situations and emotions.

Linda Francalancia-Hacker
Andover, MA

Spencer O'Dowd
Methuen, MA

TODDLER PUZZLES

You can make your own picture puzzles by mounting simple magazine pictures with a lot of straight lines on heavy cardboard. Cut the mounted picture into six or seven simple pieces and give it to your toddler to reassemble.

Julie Lapham
N. Andover, MA

SUPPER TIME WITH SMILES

We began a guessing game which has turned supper time into a much more pleasant experience and encourages conversation. In between bites, we take turns asking questions about characters from our favorite books or videos. For example, someone might ask, "What kind of animal is Eeyore?" or "Who are Thomas the Tank Engine's friends?" This game distracts our kids from noticing foods on their plate they don't like—such as peas—and often an entire dinner gets eaten in the process! We've begun to expand our conversations to how we spend our day. All you need is a sense of humor and a repertoire of children's stories.

Martha Sperandio
Andover, MA

When you are in the supermarket with children who need to be in the large part of the basket, place a hand carrier under the cart to hold perishable items.

Maria Chan
Andover, MA

My baby loves to be held up high and have her tummy rubbed on the top of my head. We've given this suggestion to her day care providers with excellent results.

Christine Lewis
Andover, MA

When a baby is just learning to sit, place a good sized rubber ball between his legs. The ball will give him some support and prevent him from falling forward.

Marlies Zammuto
Andover, MA

A playpen is a great place for your older child to escape and play with some of her "big kid" toys. In the playpen, your older child can build with blocks or create her own pretend world without worrying that her younger sibling will descend upon her at any moment.

Francine Fritsch Gikow
N. Andover, MA

If you are looking for a good child developmental newsletter with lots of practical parenting tips and age-appropriate activities, subscribe to <u>The Growing Child</u>. When you send in your order, include your child's birthdate. Each month you will receive a newsletter that is age specific (up to age six) for your child. Write to:

The Growing Child
P.O. Box 101
22 North Second Street
Lafayette, IN 47902

Tim & Marilyn Pasden
Brandon, FL

To protect a cushioned chair from a messy toddler, insert the cushion into a pillowcase. You may want to remove the pillowcase when guests are expected.

Lynne Doxsey
Andover, MA

Collect metal and plastic lids from recycled jars and containers. Keep them in a kitchen cabinet or drawer where your toddler can bring them out to stack, bang, nestle, line up, count, or sort by size or color.

Norma Villarreal
Andover, MA

Homemade rattles are easy to make. Simply pour a few dried beans into a clean plastic bottle with a screw-on safety top. This rattle may not be the most attractive one on the market, but my son loves the noise it makes and enjoys chewing on its ridged top.

Gillian Breckman
Winnipeg, Canada

If a crib or child's bed gets wet at night, place a thick towel or baby blanket over the wet spot and then change the sheets in the morning.

Maria Chan
Andover, MA

Our children learned to drink from a cup in the bathtub. From the time they were six months old, we'd give them a cup of water in the bath. At first we had to hold the cup for them as they practiced sipping from it. As they got older, they held the cup on their own and drank. They enjoyed this nightly ritual and we never had to worry about wet clothes or puddles on the floor.

Elizabeth Fletcher Foy
N. Andover, MA

Worried about getting little fingers caught in the door? Drape a bath towel over the top of the door to keep it from closing tight.

Deborah Turiano
Andover, MA

PARTY TIME:
IDEAS, GAMES, FAVORS

TOOL THEME PARTY

My four-year-old came up with his own idea for a birthday party theme - tools - and we took it from there. I made tool boxes by covering shoe boxes with brown paper and inserting twine in each corner. I joined the twine in the middle with the cardboard tube from an old hanger and we had a tool box! The kids decorated their tool-boxes with tool stickers, sten-cils, cutouts, and their own artwork.

The main party activity was making wood sculptures. I pur-chased wooden plaques and a variety of wood turnings, beads, and tiny dowel rods. Before the party, I drilled a few holes (sized to fit dowel rods, nails and screws) in each plaque. During the party, I gave each child a pile of wooden notions to glue, screw, or nail into the plaque. After each child had finished his sculpture, we took a photo of him holding his creation. We enclosed this picture in our thank you note.

Party goodies included the toolbox filled with the leftover wooden notions, a set of small tools, and the project itself.

Suzanne Knight
Andover, MA

TEA PARTY

Everyone loves a tea party! You will need tea party hats and three props for the party games described below.

PREPARATION

1) Tea Party Hat - Purchase wide brimmed straw hats for each guest plus an assortment of materials with which to decorate it, such as paper or silk flowers, feathers, satin hearts, doilies, and swatches of colored netting tied in the middle with pretty ribbon. Insert both ends of a pipe cleaner upwards through the brim of the hat so that the netting or doilies can be easily tied in place by the children.

2) Gloves - Purchase one pair of gloves for each guest from a second-hand clothing store.

3) Feather Duster - Purchase paint stirrers from a paint store and paint them pink or white. Let them dry. Using a glue gun, attach six to eight pink or black feathers at one end to create a feather duster. Make one duster for each child.

THE PARTY

While the guests are arriving, let the children decorate their hats with the materials provided. An adult with a glue gun may need to assist in gluing on certain items.

1) Tea Cup Race - Send the children to look for pairs of gloves hidden earlier in another room. Once they have returned with their gloves, divide the guests into three teams and have them put on their gloves and hat. Give the first child on each team a "cup of tea"--a paper cup filled with cotton balls--on a small paper plate. Each child must walk, while balancing her tea cup and saucer on the palm of her hand, to a table set up at the end of the room. When she reaches the table, she must set the tea cup and saucer on the table, and then pick it back up, and return to her teammates.

2) Tea Bag Race - After the tea cup race, send the children into another room in which you have hidden all of the feather dusters. Have the guests find their dusters and then return to the party room. Divide the guests into three teams and give the first child in each team a pink balloon with a tea bag tied to it. At the end of the room, place three large pots on the floor. The object of the game is to use the feather duster to push the balloon down to the pot, then scoop it into the pot, and finally, bat it back to the next team member.

When the party is over the guests may take home their decorated hat, gloves and feather duster.

Natasha Pakravan
Andover, MA

JUNGLE SAFARI PARTY

We planned this outdoor party for my daughter when she turned five. We decorated the yard with life-size jungle animals, including a monkey, a giraffe, a leopard without spots, an elephant, and a kangaroo with a baby in its pouch. We copied the animals from coloring books and sketched them with chalk on huge pieces of cardboard. After painting them, we propped up the animals on trees around the yard.

We made a lion's cave out of a huge box (4 by 4 by 8 feet) by making a large, round opening in one of its sides. Then we painted a lion on the opposite side of the box.

Using a 12-foot segment of an old dryer vent, we created a very long snake. We covered the dryer vent with brown grocery bags. Then we attached two paper bags together to make the snake's head and placed them at one end of the vent. We even stuck a forked tongue made out of red cardboard between the two paper bags. On the day of the party, we hid the snake in some thick bushes with only its head visible.

A few days before the party, we made a papier-mâché spider. We followed the instructions outlined in *Making a Piñata,* p. 156, to make the spider's body. Then we made the spider's head by stuffing a small paper bag with newspaper and attaching it to the body. Finally, we cut four slits on each side of the body and stapled a piece of black construction paper that had been rolled or folded lengthwise into the slits to make eight spider legs. We covered the head and body with black crepe paper. (You could also paint the entire piñata black.) On the day of the party, we had the following activities:

1) We played Pin the Spots on the Leopard and hunted for coconuts.

2) The kids took turns standing behind the kangaroo and putting their heads through a circular opening we'd cut out of the baby's face. (You can take a picture of each "kangaroo child" and enclose her photograph in your thank you note.) Afterward, we had a peanut toss through the opening.

3) We made spy glasses from toilet paper rolls (see Safari Binoculars, p. 60) and went on a Snake Hunt. Once the snake was sighted, we all helped pull it out of the bushes.

4) We hung the papier-mâché spider, filled with candy and treats, from a tree and placed a stool, a wooden bowl, and a spoon below it. Each child then had a turn sitting on the stool. While she was eating her curds and whey, someone would lower the spider to "frighten" the child away. We then let each child hit the piñata with a plastic bat. When the piñata broke open all the children collected goodies to take home.

Barbara Murphy
Andover, MA

SPACE FANTASY PARTY

Have an extraterrestrial experience with a Space Fantasy Party.

PREPARATION

We covered our windows with black poster board decorated with glitter and silver stars arranged in constellations. Then we hung black crepe paper, twinkling Christmas lights and stars and comets, made from silver paper and aluminum foil, from the ceiling. We made several papier-mâché meteorites by covering papier-mâché balls with foil and attaching shiny, silver streamers to represent meteorite tails. The party table was covered with aluminum foil and set with black and silver paper products.

The party was conducted in two rooms which were linked together by an "air lock." In space, an air lock is the chamber in which astronauts are able to pass from one atmospheric pressure to another. We built our air lock by shaping our Quadro (a plastic, tubular climbing structure) into a long tunnel which ended in an enlarged space approximately 4 by 4 by 4 feet. We draped heavy blankets over the "air lock" to make the passageway into space as dark as possible.

THE PARTY

To launch our space party, we handed each child a lunch bag filled with gold and silver stars, gold and silver markers, space stickers, and gold and silver glitter. Their task was to make a star map on their paper bag using the materials provided inside. When all of the children had arrived at the party and the star maps were completed, we gave each child a name tag with a planet's name written on it. For the duration of the party, each child was referred to by his planet name. We also issued each child a small flashlight. The kids held their flashlights on their journey through the air lock.

Once through the air lock and into the party room - illuminated only by flashlights and the twinkling lights overhead - the kids did the following:

1) They used a robotic arm to pick up moon rocks. The robotic arm was simply a dowel rod equipped with a string and a magnet to pick up paper clips hidden behind a barrier.

2) They did the Comet Dance - freeze dancing - to weird, synthesized outer space music.

3) They crawled back and forth through the air lock.

OUTDOOR PARTY GAMES

1) The Planet Shuffle - We placed several eight-inch-wide boards end to end and asked the children to line up on the boards. Then we instructed them to put themselves in order--without stepping off the board into outer space--from the sun to the outermost planet in the universe. The children had to figure out the planetary order and squeeze around each other to line up correctly.

2) Astronaut Training School - We set up an obstacle course that included skills such as walking on a board laid on the grass while wearing goggles fitted with bike reflectors (a favorite), digging for silver moon rocks in the sandbox, and following a string while walking backwards and looking through binoculars.

The children took home their lunch bag "star maps," flashlights, space-related candies (meteor rocks, gummi space shapes), and outer space soaps.

Suzanne Knight
Andover, MA

BUGS, BUGS, BUGS BIRTHDAY PARTY

My daughter was creator and director of her fourth birthday party theme - BUGS. Together we made lady bug invitations. She glued the spots on the ladybugs. We used fasteners so that the ladybug wings opened to the invitation.

Before the party, we painted some large bugs on heavy cardboard including a spider, a bee, an ant, and a dragonfly. We cut out these creatures and, on the day of the party, hung them outside.

The spider dangled from a tree under which we placed a kiddie pool filled with water and whiffle or golf balls. We picked up fishing nets at the Christmas Tree Shoppe. When the kids arrived they fished for "spider eggs," scooping them up out of the pool.

LADYBUG INVITATION

Next we had a bug hunt for some "not very hidden" plastic bugs. We found the bugs at the Christmas Tree Shoppe and a big pack of ants at the drugstore. After opening the presents, we brought out several "beehives" made from large cardboard boxes we had painted yellow. The kids buzzed in and out of the beehives until it was time to go home.

Instead of a goody bag, each child brought home a fishing net and some plastic bugs.

Bev Therkelsen
Andover, MA

FISH THEME PARTY

My five-year-old decided he wanted to have a party with a fish theme. We attached dark blue balloons encased in sheer fabric to all our windows to create a blue hue in the room. Blow up sharks and fish nets filled with more blue balloons hung from the ceiling. Shells decorated the table tops and humpback whale songs provided background music.

When the children arrived, they each made a fish party hat. I gave each child a 3 by 30 inch strip of poster board and let them decorate their "hats" with ocean colors, fish stickers, and their own artwork. Then I cut two notches in each child's strip. When the hats were put together, the overlapping ends resembled fish tails!

The following fish and water games went on simultaneously:

1) Some children tried to knock down stacks of paper cups using large water squirters.

2) Others went fishing using a rod with a string and magnet attached. I had cut fish from poster board, placed paper clips on their noses, and put them in a dry pool.

3) Some fishermen chose to use a plastic hook to fish for plastic fish that were swimming in a water-filled pool.

4) Others decided to try their hand at throwing fish-decorated ping pong balls into a large, glass fishbowl.

5) Each child received a wind-up fish (labeled with his name), which he entered in a fish race held in a water-filled pool.

The children received their goody bags by fishing with a rod off of our deck. My husband was below to hook on the bag and the kids reeled them in!

Suzanne Knight
Andover, MA

FISH HAT

PET SHOW PARTY

Tell all of the guests to bring their favorite stuffed animal to the party. Set up different stations around the room with activities the children can do with their animals. For example, you might have:

1) A weighing-in station equipped with a food scale.

2) A height station equipped with a yard stick.

3) A grooming station equipped with brushes and yarn for making colorful leashes.

4) A medical station equipped with a stethescope and Band-Aids for administering first-aid.

At some point during the party, have all of the guests sit in a circle and introduce their stuffed animals. Afterwards, line up the animals for judging and have an adult award an appropriate ribbon--"Biggest," "Silliest," "Most Adorable"-- to each animal. Chocolate medals, described in the next activity, make delicious awards!

Jenny Bixby
Acton, MA

CHOCOLATE MEDALS

Add a special touch to any party game by awarding the participants with these chocolate medals. Melt some chocolate in the top of a double boiler. Pour the melted chocolate into cupcake liners, just covering the bottom. Allow the chocolate to cool and then wrap each chocolate circle in foil. Cut some ribbon into one yard lengths and attach one medal to each strip of ribbon using masking tape. Store the medals in the refrigerator until you are ready to award the medals to the honorees.

Susan Russell
Andover, MA

OBSTACLE COURSE

For our daughter's summer birthday, we usually have field day races including relays, egg and spoon races, and pillow case races. This year, for her sixth birthday, we added an obstacle course to the festivities. We set up seven stations in the yard and placed a parent at each station to read rhyming instructions to the children.

We told our birthday guests that they were shipwrecked on a pirate's island. The only way to freedom was for all the guests to finish the "Survival Course" and reach the safety of the sandbox beach. Then we had the children line up at the start of the course.

Our obstacle course consisted of the following stations and rhyming instructions:

Station 1 - A canoe with a paddle and a life jacket. "Put on your lifejacket, the rest is fun. Before you know it, you'll be done. Ten strokes to go, you'll make it we know."

Station 2 - A slide. "Take an elephant ride, before a pirate's at your side."

Station 3 - A tree. "Birthday tree, skip around three." (Children must skip around the tree three times.)

Station 4 - A croquet ball and a wicket. "Knock the ball through, a credit to you."

Station 5 - A ladder lying on the ground. "Make no mistake, you're crocodile bait." (Children had to tiptoe over the ladder's rungs.)

Station 6 - A small table with a pitcher of water and small bowls. "Nature's water hole, take a sip from a bowl."

Station 7 - Three bowls of water set in a row, one foot apart. "Hop just for fun, now you are done." (Children had to hop over each bowl.)

Once all the children had made it safely to the sandbox beach, they shared a pirate's treasure box filled with gold-wrapped chocolate coins.

Mary Pritchard
Andover, MA

HOMEMADE INVITATIONS

Design your own party invitations by folding an 8½ by 11 inch piece of paper in half and writing out the invitation on the inside. (Be sure to specify that it is a *birthday* party.) Then have the birthday child decorate the invitation. Keep the outside of the folded invitation blank.

Simply design one invitation, then make as many copies as you need. Your child may choose to color or personalize each copy. Staple each invitation shut and then stick on a first class stamp. No envelope is needed!

Karen M. Sloan
Plainview, NY

MAKING A PIÑATA

flour	masking tape
bowl	tempera paint
water	paintbrush
string	newspaper
candy	large balloon
trinkets	

Blow up a large balloon and knot it. Then rip newspaper into long one-inch-wide strips. (Be sure to rip, not cut, the strips.) In a large bowl, make a flour and water paste by adding water, a 1/4 cup at a time, to two cups of flour. Continue adding water until the mixture has the liquid consistency of thick paint. Soak the strips of newspaper one at a time in the paste and

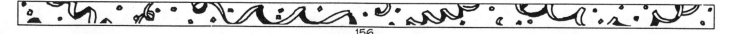

then press them onto the balloon. Overlap the strips, covering the entire surface of the balloon. Let the balloon dry for 24 hours.

When the papier-mâché balloon is completely dry, tie some string around the balloon, and tape it in place with masking tape. Be sure to leave an extra foot or so of loose string for hanging the piñata later. Next apply another layer of papier-mâché by dipping newspaper strips in a new batch of paste. Again, let the ball dry for 24 hours. (For even stronger piñatas, add additional layers of papier-mâché.)

When the piñata is completely dry, cut a hatch near the top of the balloon approximately three inches long on each side. When you make the hatch, the balloon will pop.

Decorate the piñata using tempera paint and scraps of paper or cloth. Then fill it with candy or trinkets.

At the party, hang the piñata from a broomstick and have two grownups hold it, or suspend the piñata from a swing set. A plastic bat works well for hitting the piñata. Have each child take a turn hitting it. (Older children may be blindfolded.) Be sure to keep other children away from the child taking his turn!

NOTE: This is a messy activity. Be sure to do it on a washable surface. Also, this project needs to be done several days before the party, not on the day of the party.

Denie Brand.
Andover, MA

PAPER ROLL BIRDS

paint	scissors
paper	rubber band
glitter	glue or stapler
markers	toilet paper roll
feathers	construction paper

Paper roll birds add spark to a party table. Make one for each child at the party. First cut two 1/2 inch slits on each end of a toilet paper roll, positioning the four slits across from each other. Use the slits to stretch a rubber band from one end of the toilet paper roll to the other, forming a rectangular shape. When plucked, the rubber band will give the bird its twangy bird call. Paint the bird's paper roll body or cover it with construction paper.

Draw two wings on another piece of construction paper, allowing a 1/2 inch border to glue or staple the wings onto the body. Cut out the wings and decorate them with markers, glitter, or feathers. Then attach the wings to the back of the bird's body.

Next draw a beak on construction paper. Cut it out and fold it in half lengthwise. Make a notch in the center of the wide end of the beak and make a 1/4 inch fold on either side where the beak can be attached to the bird.

Glue or tape the beak in place on the bird's body. Cut out two feet from construction paper and make a 1/2 inch fold where the feet will be attached to the body. Glue or staple the feet in place along the fold line. Use buttons, pompoms, or markers to make the bird's eyes.

Diane Paff
Andover, MA

TREASURE CHESTS

Treasure chests are a popular party activity. Use one of the following variations to prepare the chests before the party.

SHOE BOX CHESTS

glue	collage materials
shoe boxes	rope/pipe cleaners
spray paint	

Collect and spray paint a shoe box for each party guest. If you don't have enough shoe boxes, local shoe stores are usually happy to help out.

Punch two level holes on both ends of the box and loop a piece of rope or a pipe cleaner through each set of holes to make handles. Secure the rope handles by knotting them. Decorate the chest as described below.

MILK CARTON CHESTS

paper bags
collage materials
paper towel rolls
1/2 gal. paper milk cartons (clean)

Fold down the pointed end of a half-gallon paper milk carton to make two flat ends. Using a pair of scissors, cut a three-sided flap opening in one of the sides of the carton. Glue two paper towel rolls, cut to size, to the flap. Cover the entire outer surface with brown paper from paper bags. The chest should now appear to have a rounded cover.

On the day of the party, the children can decorate their chests using junky jewelry, sequins, pompoms, buttons, colored glue, colored macaroni, glitter, shiny fabric, colored paper clips, stickers, and brightly colored ribbon.

Kathy DiTroia
N. Andover, MA

Leslie Silverstein
Andover, MA

BALLOON PEOPLE

glue	sunglasses
hats	large balloons
stickers	construction paper

Creating balloon people is a great party activity for older children.

Before the party, cut out various shapes from construction paper to use as eyes, noses, mouths and eyebrows.

On the day of the party tie large balloons to chairs and let the children decorate the balloon people with the paper shapes. Have plenty of hats, sunglasses, and other funny accessories on hand for the finishing touch.

My living room was filled with balloon people after our party. When my husband arrived home, he had a good laugh when he discovered the "company" in our living room.

Liat Weiler
Philadelphia, PA

EDIBLE NECKLACES

lacing   shoestring licorice
Froot Loops, or other "string-able" cereal

Stringing cereal on lacing or shoestring licorice is a party craft that children of all ages can enjoy. Stiffer plastic lacing (found in craft stores) is especially easy for younger children to thread. Cut lacing into 20-inch lengths and make a knot at one end. Give a string of lacing or licorice to each child along with a pile of Froot Loops. When she has finished stringing, tie the two ends together to make a colorful and tasty necklace.

Marcia Strykowski
Bradford, MA

DECORATED CHAIRS

For my daughter's third birthday, I bought inexpensive plastic chairs for children (sold at K-Mart or Ames) and decorated them. First, I wrote each child's name on her chair and then I drew pictures of something that child liked, for example, dinosaurs, stars, the sun, or flowers. At the party, each child used her own chair in a game of musical chairs.

For the record, we were not very successful with the music or the children's attention. In any case, each child got to take her own chair home.

Ethel Schuster
Andover, MA

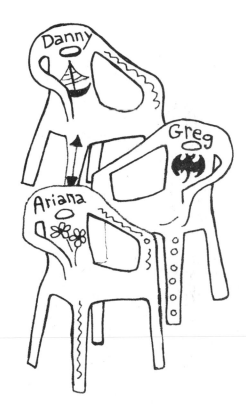

SHADOW BLOCKS

blocks	paper
flashlight	crayons/paint

Have the guests build a structure out of blocks. Place a large piece of white paper on the wall behind the structure. Turn off the lights and shine a flashlight on the blocks. The light will cast a shadow on the white paper, which the children can trace. Then lay the paper on the floor and let them color or paint the unusual design.

Mel Damphousse
Andover Community Child Care Center
Andover, MA

SURPRISE BOX

This activity gives everyone a present to unwrap. You will need a party favor and box for each guest. The boxes must increase in size from very small to very large. Place the first gift inside the smallest box, wrap this box, then place it with

another gift inside the next larger box. Wrap this box and continue the process until all of the boxes and gifts are in one large box.

At the party, have the guests sit in a circle. Turn on some music and have the children pass the large box around the circle. When the music stops, the child holding the box unwraps it, takes the gift, and then leaves the circle. The children continue to pass the box in the same way until the last guest gets the smallest wrapped box.

Marie Haley
Andover, MA

PICTURE FRAMES

stickers   self adhesive letters
poster board

Before the party, cut out 8 by 10 inch rectangles from colored poster board. To make the frames, cut out a rectangular-shaped center in each piece of poster board slightly smaller than a standard-size photo or a particular piece of artwork. Using self-adhesive vinyl letters, put each party guest's name on a frame.

On the day of the party, give each child an assortment of stickers with which to decorate her frame. Buttons can also be glued around the frames for a unique look.

Beth Barwick
Andover, MA

WATER RELAY RACE

4 large bowls	water
2 sponges	

This is a great summer relay race especially when your party guests are wearing swimsuits. The object of the relay race is to transfer water from one bowl to another using a sponge.

Divide the children into two teams. Place a large bowl of water in front of each team with a large sponge in each bowl. Place an empty bowl approximately 25 feet away from each team. At the word, "Go," the first two children grab the water-soaked sponges and race down to their team's empty bowl. Each child squeezes the water out of her sponge and into the empty bowl. Then she races back to her team and the next child in line soaks her sponge and repeats the process. The first team to transfer all of the water from the full bowl to the empty bowl is the winner.

Susan Russell
Andover, MA

PARTY RELAY GAME

This is our favorite party relay game because there are no apparent winners or losers. It is also adaptable to any season or occasion: for a Valentine's Day party, use heart shapes; for a party in the fall, use pumpkins.

In preparation for a summertime version of this game, cut out twelve 10-inch fish shapes, six fish for each team. On each of the fish in each set, write a different command, such as SKIP, HOP, RUN, DUCK WALK, FROG LEAP, or RUN BACKWARDS.

On the day of the party, divide the children into two teams. Place two adults at the far end of the room with each team's stack of fish. At the word, "Go," one child from each group runs up to the stack of fish, an adult reads the command on the first fish, and the child returns to her teammates by hopping, running, or leaping. Once the relay is underway, the children soon lose track of who is ahead, focusing instead on their next turn to run, hop, or jump.

Mary Pritchard
Andover, MA

FOREST PARTY GAME

Place some chairs in a circle using one less chair than the number of children. Give each child a piece of notepaper with an animal stamp or sticker on it. Be sure each child's stamp is different. Then make a master list with all of the stamps or stickers on it. Using the master list, the birthday child begins the game by standing in the middle of the circle and calling out two of the stamp animals, for example, "panda" and "tiger." The two children holding those two animal stamps rush for each other's chair while the birthday child does the same.

Whoever is left without a chair stands in the middle and takes a turn calling out two animals on the sheet. Any child in the center may decide not to call out two animals but instead to call out "Forest Party." This signals all the children to jump up in a free-for-all exchange of places.

Linda Pakravan
Andover, MA

SQUEAL, PIGGY, SQUEAL

Squeal, Piggy, Squeal is a common party game in England. Have children sit in a circle. Then pick one person to be "it." Blindfold that child and have him sit in the middle of the circle. Turn on some music and tell the children in the circle to stand up and walk around the circle. When the music stops, everyone should sit back down in the circle and the person in the middle should sit in someone's lap. The lap person squeals and the blindfolded child tries to guess whose lap he is sitting on.

Claudia Simon
Andover, MA

OPERATOR! OPERATOR!

Have the children sit on the floor in a circle. The birthday child starts the game by whispering a message to the child sitting next to her. The message is whispered from child to child until it arrives at the last person who repeats it out loud. It is fun to hear how much the message has changed from the first to the last child. You might start the game with this message - "Mrs. Bogs needs a bag." - and end the game with this message - "It's time to sing Happy Birthday."

Natasha Pakravan
Andover, MA

PIN THE POINT ON THE CRAYON

tape	construction paper
blindfold	colored poster board
scissors	

Cut out a large rectangle from colored poster board. Draw a crayon, without a point, on the rectangle. Then cut out points from different colored construction paper. Place some rolled up tape on the back of each point. Then have the children take turns being blindfolded to Pin the Point on the Crayon.

You can tailor this classic party game to almost any party theme. For example, if you are having a Wild West Party, you might play Pin the Hat on the Cowboy.

Beth Barwick
Andover, MA

GOODY BAG HUNT

This is a great hunt for an indoor party. Assemble all the goody bag items and divide them into separate piles, one pile per child. Wrap each item individually with tissue paper and put an identifying sticker or stamp on each one. Each child's goody bag items should have the same stamp. Then put the correlating stamp or sticker on a paper bag. For example, one child will be given a paper bag with a unicorn stamp on it. When the hunt begins, that child will be hunting only for little presents with a unicorn stamp on it. Hide one item per room so that when the child has discovered her unicorn in a particular room, she moves onto the next room to hunt for another unicorn-labeled item.

Or hide goody bags outside and have the children hunt for their bags as they leave the party.

Linda Pakravan
Andover, MA

SPIDER WEB
GRAB BAG HUNT

I have fond childhood memories of this activity - I'm crawling on my hands and knees following this piece of string under tables and over couches until my string leads me to a wrapped-up coloring book hidden in the piano seat. As a parent, I couldn't wait for my children to be old enough to follow their own strings. We did our spider web hunt outside but it can work indoors if you don't have too many guests.

Wrap yards of string around some popsicle sticks, one for each guest. Place each popsicle stick at the starting point and then lay out a course as complicated or interesting as possible - around trees, down slides, under bushes. Your lawn will look like a spider's web. (Try to avoid overlapping the string in one course with that in another, because they may become tangled together during the hunt.)

While the course is being laid out, all the children can be gathered in another room playing Simon Says. When the hunt begins, have each child follow her string, wrapping it back on to the popsicle stick as she goes, until she discovers her hidden goody bag.

Mary Pritchard
Andover, MA

SURPRISE PARTY PACKAGE

glue	small gifts
scissors	toilet paper rolls
stickers	colored crepe paper

Surprise party packages make wonderful favors and can be filled with either small gifts or candy.

Cut a 14 by 20 inch piece of crepe paper or construction paper for each toilet paper roll. Center the roll along the long edge of the paper and glue the roll to the paper. Then glue the rest of the paper around the roll leaving approximately four inches of paper sticking out past both ends of the roll. Cut this excess paper into a fringe. (See diagram.) Then insert candy or gifts inside the roll, twist the paper at both ends, and tie them with some ribbon. Decorate each party package with stickers and markers.

Diane Paff
Andover, MA

glue roll to paper

cut fringe

twist ends after inserting gift

CANDY TRAIN FAVORS

1 pkg. gum	1 roll of Life Savers
Hershey Kiss	4 peppermint pinwheels

Use the above <u>individually wrapped</u> ingredients to make an edible candy train. To assemble the train, place the Life Savers roll on the long, flat side of the package of gum and glue them together. Then glue on the wrapped peppermint pinwheels as the wheels, and the Hershey's Kiss as the smoke stack. A glue gun makes this process easier and longer lasting.

Susan Russell
Andover, MA

GIFT CERTIFICATES

My daughter's birthday is in January and there really isn't much she needs after all of the holiday gift giving. As we were discussing what to buy her last year, my husband recalled how proud she was to give us homemade gift certificates, (for setting the table or washing the dishes), and how much she enjoyed having us use them. We decided to reciprocate.

Our gift certificates were a tremendous hit! They underscored what a great gift she had given us, and she had control over when to use them. Examples of our gift certificates included staying up a half hour later one night, choosing a rental video whenever she wanted, and a night without vegetables for dinner. We felt a bit like *Little House on the Prairie* with our homemade gifts, but it helped us focus on the celebration of the person.

Nancy Kendrick
Andover, MA

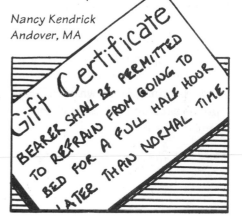

Gift Certificate
BEARER SHALL BE PERMITTED TO REFRAIN FROM GOING TO BED FOR A FULL HALF HOUR LATER THAN NORMAL TIME.

My one-year-old daughter, Anna, and I decorate paper grocery bags with crayons and stickers and use them as wrapping paper. They make a distinctive package for a child's birthday present!

Kathy Whelan
Methuen, MA

We often use newspaper as wrapping paper - comics for children and appropriate sections for other family members and friends. For example, we wrap a present for a sports enthusiast with the sports section's headline visible on front of the package.

Margaret Dhaliwal   *Andrew Fletcher*
Andover, MA   *New York, NY*

Before a birthday party, fill a large trash bag with enough blown up balloons for each party guest. When your child is ready to open his gifts, open this bag of balloons first. Pass out the balloons to the children so that each child has a balloon to hold while your child opens his presents. (<u>Caution:</u> Do not do this activity with children who are still putting things in their mouths!)

Nancy Laorenza
N. Andover, MA

Instead of taking time to decorate cupcakes for birthday parties, let each child decorate his own. Give each child a three section piece of egg carton filled with sprinkles, colored sugars, chocolate chips or other decorating materials. Place each cupcake in a paper bowl, to contain the mess, and then stand back and enjoy the fun.

Sue Siegel
Andover, MA

Use a bicycle pump to make blowing up balloons easier.

Jeremy Foy
N. Andover, MA

Make a family or birthday time capsule to open in the year 2000 or to open on your child's 21st birthday.

Mary Pritchard
Andover, MA

Make a wrapped present even more festive by using crepe paper for the ribbon and feathers for the bow.

Bev Therkelsen
Andover, MA

At birthday parties, make "losers" feel like winners while playing games, such as musical chairs or hot potato, by cheering for them or giving them a small party favor as they step out of the game.

Lee Hartzell
Andover, MA

An annual birthday interview is a special way to watch your child grow over the years. Record the interview on a video or audio cassette that is reserved just for these annual interviews. You and your child will enjoy looking back on these interviews in the years to come.

Patti Meade
Andover, MA

To help parents become familiar with the name of each guest, have each child write his name on a name tag when he first arrives. Then have him decorate the name tag and stick it on his shirt.

Nancy Johnson
Andover, MA

Decorating cookies is one of our favorite party activities. Using cookie cutters, I make at least two cookies per child--one to eat at the party and one to bring home. The children decorate their cookies with frosting, sprinkles, raisins, nuts, and chocolate chips.

Nancy Laorenza
N. Andover, MA

SEASONAL IDEAS

DRESS-UP SCARECROW

1 bale of hay	1 3-ft. piece of wood
dress-up clothes	1 4-ft. piece of wood

Invite an older sibling or willing teenager to be dressed up as a scarecrow. If the volunteer is tall, he will need to kneel on the ground so that the children can dress and stuff him with hay.

Drive a four-foot piece of wood into the ground and nail a three-foot crosspiece of wood to it. The scarecrow's arms can then be "tied" to the crosspiece which also provides a place for the scarecrow's arms to rest. Pile some dress-up clothes next to the scarecrow. Be sure to include hats, scarves, aprons, skirts, and frills.

Once the scarecrow has been properly attired by the children, let them stuff him with hay. (Be sure to solicit a scarecrow who doesn't mind a little hay under the collar.) Gather the children around their scarecrow for a good photo opportunity.

Mary Pritchard
Andover, MA

APPLE AND PUMPKIN PICKING

Every fall, our family visits one of the many local farms to pick apples and select a few pumpkins. We make a special apple-picking device to reach up high into the tree. First we cut a two-liter soda bottle in half around the middle, keeping the half with the spout end. Then we stick a broomstick into the spout and secure it in place with duct tape. When apple picking, we use this device to reach high up into the tree. Just knock an apple gently and it will fall into the bottle scoop.

Pat Picard
Andover, MA

PAPIER-MÂCHÉ PUMPKINS

water	string
flour	newspaper
paint	large balloons

Make a piñata as described in *Making a Piñata* on p. 156. Once the piñata is dry, let your child decorate it to look like a pumpkin with tempera paint and paper or cloth scraps. Make a hole on each side of the pumpkin near the top and insert some string for a handle. Use the papier-mâché pumpkin for trick or treat or as a decoration!

Maura Santos
Peabody, MA

EDIBLE TURKEYS

apple	gummy worms
orange	small marshmallows
toothpicks	large marshmallows
gumdrops	

Turkeys are easy for children to assemble and they taste good too. Give each child an apple or orange for the turkey's body and toothpicks for the head, legs, and tail feathers. Use a large marshmallow for the head, a gummy worm for the wattle, and small marshmallows for the legs. Decorate the tail feather toothpicks with a colorful assortment of gumdrops.

Maureen MacRae
Andover, MA

HOLIDAY TABLECLOTH

For a beautiful holiday dinner table, spread a plain red tablecloth on your dining room table. Arrange your children's artwork on top. Small cutout paper snowflakes or lace doily hearts (depending on the holiday) can be added to balance out the design. Then cover their artwork with a clear vinyl tablecloth. This project keeps children busy for quite a while and they are very proud of the results.

Marcia Strykowski
Bradford, MA

MAKE A MENORAH

The lighting of the Menorah is a beautiful ceremony marking the Festival of Lights. There are nine candles in the Menorah - one for each of the eight nights of Chanukah and one for the Shamas, the "attendant" candle, which is used to light the other candles. Make one of the following Menorahs to celebrate this religious tradition:

PAPER MENORAH

nine straws	yellow tissue paper
construction paper	

To make a paper Menorah, cut out a Menorah shape and glue it onto a piece of construction paper. Cut eight of the colored straws the same length. Cut the ninth straw, the Shamas, slightly longer than the others. Glue the colored straws in any order on the Menorah, placing the Shamas in the middle. Light one candle for each night of Chanukah by gluing crumpled yellow tissue paper onto each straw. The Shamas remains lit for all eight nights.

THREE-DIMENSIONAL MENORAH

play dough	art supplies
paper plates	birthday candles

To make a three-dimensional Menorah, decorate a paper plate using anything from markers and glitter to marshmallows and sugar cubes. Then arrange nine small balls of play dough on the decorated paper plate. Make one ball larger than the others to represent the Shamas. Place one birthday candle into each of the play dough balls. This Menorah may be purely decorational or lit with discretion.

Jody Brickman
Andover, MA

CHANUKAH PAPER CHAINS

construction paper:	scissors
blue and white	stapler or glue

Cut blue and white construction paper into 1 by 8 inch strips. Then help your children make paper chains to decorate the room. Be sure to alternate the colors in each chain.

NOTE: By simply changing the colors of the chain, you can adapt this activity to other holidays. For example, on Halloween, you could make orange and black chains.

Congregation Tifereth Israel
Religious School
Andover, MA

MITZVAH COUPON BOOK

markers	magazines
glue stick	construction paper

To encourage children to think of others during Chanukah, help them make a "mitzvah coupon book." A mitzvah is essentially a *deed* done to help another person. Younger children can find pictures in magazines of things they can do to be helpful, such as feeding the dog, playing with a younger sibling, or sharing toys with a friend. Help them cut out the pictures and then glue each one onto a piece of paper precut into a "coupon."

Older children can think of meaningful gifts for friends and family and design their own coupons.

Making mitzvah coupon books could be a family project, where everyone makes a coupon for each member of the family. Then one night of Chanukah is set aside for exchanging these very special gifts.

Sharon Cores
N. Reading, MA

CHRISTMAS CARD ADVENT CALENDAR

glue	rubber cement
ribbon	wrapping paper
scissors	red and green felt
hole punch	old Christmas cards
small bells	

We recycle old Christmas cards by using them to make a different type of advent calendar. Trace a 3-inch diameter circle around your favorite portion of 24 old Christmas cards. Cut these circles out of the cards. Then cut an equal number of 3-1/2 inch diameter circles from green and red felt. Glue the back of the Christmas card circles on to the felt circles. The felt circle should overlap the card circle by 1/4 inch all the way around.

Make holes at the top of each felt-backed card using a hole punch. Cut two lengths of ribbon and begin to thread 12 of the felt-backed cards onto each ribbon. After threading the first felt-backed card onto the ribbon, hold it in place by knotting the ribbon on either side of the card. Continue adding felt-backed cards to the ribbon. Space them out along the ribbon and knot the ribbon on either side of the cards to hold them in place.

Once the felt-backed cards are secured in place on each of

the ribbons, cut twenty-four 3-1/2 inch diameter circles from Christmas wrapping paper. Using rubber cement, carefully glue the back of each wrapping paper circle to the felt at the top of each felt-backed card. (Be careful not to glue the wrapping paper circle to the Christmas card.) Use a marker to label the wrapping paper flaps from 1 to 24.

Now your advent calendar is ready to hang. Your children can count the days to Christmas by lifting and/or peeling off the appropriately numbered flaps and exposing the picture beneath.

Jodi Templer
Tewksbury, MA

CHRISTMAS CARD PICTURE BOOKS

glue	hole punch
ribbon	old Christmas cards
scissors	

My children and I have enjoyed making picture books from old Christmas cards. We cut or tear off the front of each card. Then we use a hole punch to make two holes along the outside edge of each card. Using colorful ribbon, we tie the cards together.

We've sorted the cards by theme - religious, animals, and Santas - to make different books. You could also make up a story or text and write it on the bottom of each page. These books have always lasted long after the Christmas season.

Jodi Templer
Tewksbury, MA

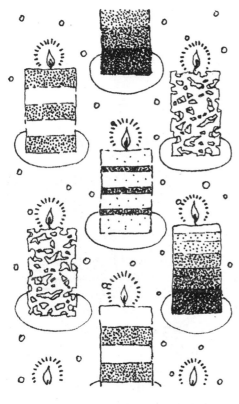

MAKE YOUR OWN CANDLES

wax blocks	pencil
candlewicks	crayons
milk cartons	oatmeal cartons

When my four children were young, I encouraged them to make Christmas presents for friends and family. One of their favorite activities was candle making. This activity requires close adult supervision, but even a two-year-old can select the colors and shapes of his candles.

First melt a block of wax in a double boiler. (NEVER melt wax directly over a flame because it is flammable!) Have your child select a crayon and add it to the wax. While the wax is melting, select a mold such as a milk carton cut in half (or any other container that can be peeled away). Tie one end of a wick around a pencil. Center the wick in the mold by resting the pencil on the mold's rim. The wick should just touch the bottom of the mold. Place the mold on top of newspaper to protect your counter from spills.

MULTICOLORED CANDLES

Carefully pour a layer of colored wax into the mold. Allow the wax to harden. Repeat this step using a different color of wax each time until your candle reaches the rim of the mold. Once the candle has hardened, your child can peel away the carton.

ICE CUBE CANDLES

After centering the wick, pour enough melted wax into the mold to create a one-inch, solid base. After the wax has cooled, fill the mold with small ice cubes or ice chips. You need to melt enough wax this time to completely fill the mold. Pour the colored wax over the ice. When the wax has hardened, peel the carton away and behold a swiss cheese-type candle. When the ice melts, it leaves holes in the candle.

At Christmas time, our kitchen was always filled with candles in various stages of completion.
Audrey Fletcher
Brentwood, NH

THE DOLL'S NEW CLOTHES

One of my favorite memories of Santa was the Christmas Eve he sneaked into my room while I was asleep and dressed my favorite doll that I slept with in a brand new, gorgeous outfit. He even neatly folded my doll's old outfit and placed it at the end of my bed. When I awoke, my doll was still in my arms dressed in her new Christmas outfit. What a thrill!

Patti Meade
Andover, MA
(In dedication to her late mother, Helen Meade)

CHRISTMAS ANGEL ORNAMENT

ribbon	scallop shells
1/2 in. lace	wooden beads
markers	cellophane ribbon
glue gun	glittery pipe cleaners

At our house, Christmas is the season of glue-filled afternoons. Ornaments, wreaths, and homemade gifts are in a constant state of production. One of our favorite ornaments is the Christmas Angel.

To begin, draw a face on a wooden bead with a marker and then glue the bead onto the top of a scallop shell. (Make a 1/4-inch collar of glue to secure the bead onto the shell.) Next, glue lace on the bottom of the shell. Decorate the scallop shell "dress" with markers and glitter. Form a pipe cleaner into a halo and attach it to the Angel's head by inserting it into the hole in the top of the bead. Cut some cellophane ribbon (or any material suitable for wings) into the shape of two wings and glue them onto the back of the shell. Position the wings at "shoulder" height. You can make a hanger by gluing a loop of ribbon onto the back of the shell.

Susan Russell
Andover, MA

STRING ORNAMENTS

glue	clothespin
string	pipe cleaner
glitter	small balloon
hanger	undiluted starch
paintbrush	

I did this project with my mother when I was a child. Blow up a small balloon to the size of a tree ornament. Unravel string, two feet at a time, and place it in a bowl of undiluted starch. Once it is soaked, pull a few inches of string out of the bowl, squeeze off excess starch and then begin wrappping the wet string randomly around the balloon. Continue to remove string from the bowl, a few inches at a time (so that it doesn't get tangled) and wrapping it around the balloon until the balloon is completely covered. Insert a safety pin into the tied end of the balloon and fasten it to a clothes hanger. Be careful not to pop the balloon. Hang the string ball over the tub (in case it drips) for approximately 24 hours. When it is dry, paint it with white glue and roll it in glitter. Pop the balloon inside the ornament and remove it. Fasten a pipe cleaner to the ornament and hang it on your tree.

Marcia S. Mucci
Methuen, MA

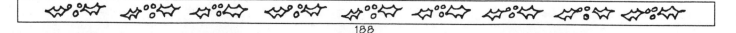

CHRISTMAS CENTERPIECE

paper plate	glue or glue gun
nature objects	votive or tea candle
gold spray paint	

This is a simple holiday centerpiece that children can help create. Before beginning this project, take a nature walk with your children and collect objects of various textures and shapes, such as pinecones, acorns, berries, pods, twigs, and evergreen branches.

Spray a paper plate with gold paint. Glue a votive candle in the center of the plate.

Arrange and glue an assortment of your outdoor treasures around the candle. Glitter and sequins can also be added. Light the finished centerpiece on Christmas Eve.

Susan Russell
Andover, MA

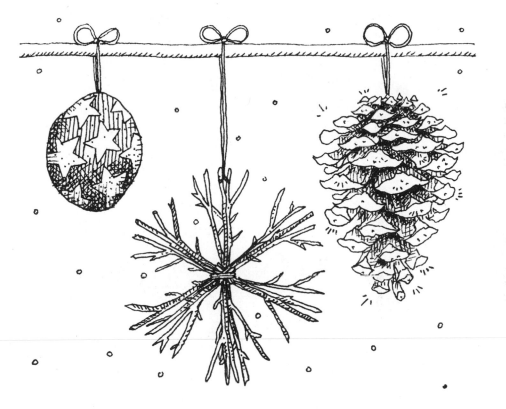

NATURAL ORNAMENTS

Create natural Christmas tree ornaments by hunting outdoors for interesting items. Spruce up pinecones with a few dots of glue and a sprinkle of glitter. Decorate small, smooth stones with markers or paint. Fashion snowflakes out of twigs by tying them together with yarn. Tie or glue string to each ornament for hanging. Be sure to attach a small piece of paper to each ornament with the child's name and date.

Cheryl Torres
Methuen, MA

POPSICLE STICK ORNAMENTS

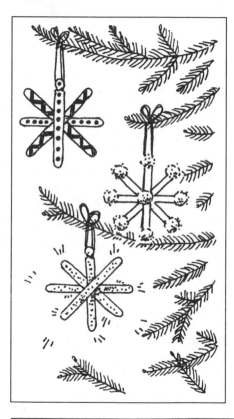

This is a fun ornament for a child of any age to make. Arrange four popsicle sticks into a star shape and then glue the sticks in place. Let your child decorate his star using various art supplies, such as glue glitter, paints, or colored pompoms. Put two notches near the end of one stick, tie a string around the notches, and hang the dried ornament on your Christmas tree.

Susan Ickes
Andover, MA

PLASTIC MELT ORNAMENTS

plastic cups	plastic beads
cookie sheet	thread
aluminum foil	cake tester

Plastic melt ornaments make colorful tree or mobile decorations and are simple to make. Put clear, plastic cups on a cookie sheet lined with aluminum foil. Have your child sprinkle colorful plastic beads or other plastic decorative materials into the cups. Place the cookie sheet in a 300° F oven and watch the cups melt.

Once the cups have melted (it doesn't take long), remove the tray from the oven. Immediately use a cake tester to make a hole at the top of each ornament. Be sure to warn your children not to touch the plastic until it cools!

When the ornaments have cooled, help your children tie thread through the holes. The ornaments are now ready to hang on your Christmas tree or wrap as a gift.

Audrey Fletcher
Brentwood, NH

SANTA ORNAMENT

glue	thread
walnut	nonpareils
red felt	cotton balls

I've enjoyed seeing the Santa ornament I made as a child hanging from our family Christmas tree for the past 24 years!

Make Santa's hat by cutting some red felt into two triangles small enough to fit over the top of a walnut. Sew two edges of the triangles together. Then glue some cotton around the base of the hat and put a cotton ball on its top. Place the hat on top of the walnut and glue it in place.

To make Santa's face, shape some cotton pieces into a mustache and beard. Glue them onto the walnut surface. Use candies to make the eyes, a nose and a mouth.

When all the glue is dry, attach some thread to the top of the hat and hang the ornament on your tree.

Diana Elser
Boston, MA

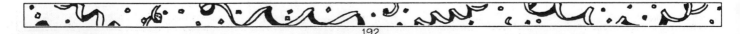

PAPER LANTERNS

Children can celebrate the Chinese New Year by making paper lanterns for decorations. Have your children decorate a rectangular piece of paper (9 by 12 inches or 8 1/2 by 11 inches) with markers, crayons, or paint. (For variety, use wallpaper to make lanterns with interesting patterns.) Then fold the paper in half lengthwise and cut fifteen to twenty 3 1/2-inch slits along the folded edge. Begin cutting about one inch from each short edge and leave 1/2 inch between each slit. Unfold the paper and tape or staple it lengthwise into a diamond-shaped cylinder. Add a 1/2 by 6 inch strip of paper to form a handle. Illuminate the lanterns with small flashlights and hang them around your house.

Vivian Lo
Hong Kong

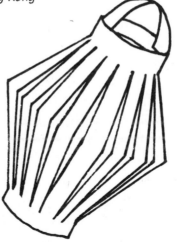

EGG CARTON DRAGON

glue	ice pick
markers	pipe cleaners
scissors	colored popcorn
egg carton	construction paper

Cut an egg carton in half lengthwise. Cut out 36 nickle-sized circles from construction paper and save them. Using markers, have your child draw colorful designs on one of the egg carton strips. Then poke holes along both sides of the decorated strip and have your child insert one 1 1/2-inch pipe cleaner into each of these holes to make the dragon's legs. Make the dragon's head by cutting one section off of the other strip and attaching it to the body with a pipe cleaner. Have your child attach four 3-inch pipe cleaners to the dragon's head and then glue on two pieces of colored popcorn to make its eyes. Make the dragon's tail by twisting five 3-inch pipe cleaners around a full-length pipe cleaner and then attaching it to the dragon. Now have your child glue two circles, back-to-back, onto each end of the pipe cleaners on the dragon's head and tail.

Vivian Lo
Hong Kong

FORTUNE COOKIE FUN

3 egg whites	1/2 c. cake flour
1/2 c. sugar	1/2 tsp. vanilla
1/4 c. brown sugar	

Help your children write 24 personalized messages on strips of paper. Preheat the oven to 350° F. Put all the ingredients in a food processor and blend for 10 to 15 seconds. Cover a cookie sheet with greased parchment paper. Make four cookies at a time by dropping measured teaspoon-fuls onto the paper. Bake the cookies for 10 minutes. Using a spatula, immediately remove the now flat cookies from the tray and place them, rough side down, on a cutting board. Put a fortune in the middle of each cookie and fold the cookies in half. Then turn the corners of each cookie up. Repeat until batter is gone. (If you work fast, or have little hands helping you, you can make more than four cookies at a time. Experiment with the timing because the dough gets hard to work with after a few minutes.) Then, let the oven cool to 200° F. Put all the shaped cookies back on the cookie sheet and bake them for approximately 30 minutes, or until completely brown.

Barbara Moverman
N. Andover, MA

HEART POUCHES

red felt	white yarn
hole punch	darning needle

Fill these pouches with candy on Valentine's Day. To make one heart pouch, cut two 4 by 4 inch hearts from red felt. Place the hearts on top of one another and use a hole punch to make holes around the heart 1/2 to 3/4 inches apart. Give your child a darning needle with the yarn tied around it and help her stitch the two hearts together. Leave enough yarn at the top of the pouch to tie it shut with a bow.

Mary Pritchard
Andover, MA

VALENTINE MAGNETS

glue	poster board
scissors	red or pink felt
strip magnet	collage materials

Cut heart shapes of equal size out of poster board and felt. Then glue them together. Let your child decorate the heart with materials, such as glitter, sequins, macaroni, and feathers. Glue a strip magnet onto the back of the decorated heart to complete the project. This project can be adapted to any season. Make a snowman magnet in the winter or a fish magnet in the summer.

Emily Tremaine
Spokane, WA

VALENTINE MOBILE

felt	glue
scissors	glitter
pine cones	thread
posterboard	sequins
fallen tree branch	stickers

Ask your child to search for a fallen branch outside that is large enough to have many items dangling from it. Over the course of several weeks, let your children and their friends add different types of valentines to it. Here are a few suggestions to give your mobile variety:

1) Collect and dry some pine cones. Paint them with glue and roll them in glitter. Tie them onto the branch with thread of varying lengths.

2) Cut out different sized heart shapes from poster board or thin cardboard. Use these shapes to trace hearts

onto red, pink, white, and purple felt. Glue the felt onto both sides of the cardboard hearts. Decorate the felt hearts with stickers, smaller felt hearts and sequins, or other collage materials.

3) Make birds using felt-covered poster board shapes. Decorate the birds with paints, markers, or feathers.

When your children's mobile is hanging above the kitchen table, February seems a much brighter month.

Mary Pritchard
Andover, MA

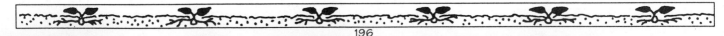

FORCING FORSYTHIA

Forsythia bushes bloom early in the spring. You can coax these buds to open earlier by bringing them inside. Help your child cut some branches from a forsythia bush. Have her peel the ends of the branches to help them absorb water. Place the branches in water. Be sure to change the water frequently. Within a few weeks, the bright yellow blossoms should open.

Note: For variety, try forcing apple blossoms, lilac bushes, and azaleas.

Barbara Hartrich
N. Andover, MA

FROM PIT TO PLANT

Have your child peel the brown covering off an avocado pit and put toothpicks around its middle. Suspend the pit, pointed side up, over a glass jar filled with water. Be sure to keep the base of the pit covered with water. Your children can observe the roots growing out of the base of the pit and a stem with leaves growing out of its top. Transplant the young plant to a pot of soil and watch it grow into a bushy plant.

Note: A sweet potato will also sprout in this manner.

Audrey Fletcher
Brentwood, NH

RITES OF SPRING

seeds	cups
seed catalogues	dirt

Each spring, my daughter invites a friend over to our house for a special afternoon. I give each child three cups to fill with dirt and let them select seeds to plant in their cups.

We look through seed catalogues to see what their seeds will look like as grown plants. It's nice for the friend to be able to take her cups of planted seeds home. It's spring!

Susan Bourland
Andover, MA

SPRING EQUINOX EVENT

We love to celebrate the beginning of the growing season and have started a tradition of a Spring Equinox party to welcome the season.

This past season, we had three events. First, we had each child plant marigold seeds in little containers. Then, we played a circle game we had read about in <u>Festivals, Family and Food</u> by Diana Carey and Judy Large called Lady Spring. The children circle around and chant:

"Look who is here
It's Lady Spring
Lady Spring, Lady Spring
Look who's here

It's Lady Spring
Lady Spring is here.

Who'll come into
Our wee ring . . .
(repeat three times)
And dance with Lady Spring?

Who'll come into
our wee ring
[Child's name] will come into
Our wee ring
(repeat three times)
[Child's name] will come into
our wee ring
To dance with Lady Spring."

The child who dances with Lady Spring then becomes Lady Spring in the next round until all of the children have had a chance to be Lady Spring and to wear her homemade gold crown.

Our final event was lighting six hand-rolled beeswax candles for a round of Happy Birthday to Lady Spring.

Elizabeth Rose
Georgetown, MA

Marsha Janson
Hamilton, MA

Maura Santos
Peabody, MA

CHOCOLATE MATZOS

4 matzos	wax paper
1 tsp. butter	baking sheet
12 oz. semi-sweet morsels	

Melt the chocolate and butter in a double boiler while your children break the matzos into small pieces. Pour the melted chocolate over the pieces and stir until they are evenly coated. Scoop the mixture onto a baking sheet covered with wax paper and pat it down into a thin layer. Refrigerate. Break the hardened chocolate matzo into small pieces and serve.

Sharon Cores
N. Reading, MA

BUNNIES IN THE GRASS

pompoms	hardboiled eggs
cardboard	paper scraps
markers/paint	fabric scraps
Easter grass	

Let your child draw or paint a bunny face onto a hard-boiled egg. Together make the bunny's ears, tail and other features using paper or fabric scraps and pompoms. Cut a small circle out of cardboard and let your child glue his bunny and some Easter grass onto it. Make a whole family of bunnies to decorate your house or garden.

Shelley Selwyn
Andover, MA

STAINED GLASS BUNNIES

oil	red Jell-O powder
scissors	pink tissue paper
wax paper	yellow tissue paper
paintbrush	

This is a simple and satisfying play group activity for the two-and three-year-old set.

Cut out one nine-inch bunny shape per child from wax paper and 20 to 25 one-to two-inch rectangles from pink and yellow tissue paper. Pour some oil into a small dish and add approximately one teaspoon of red Jell-O powder to the oil. Coloring the oil with Jell-O will help the children see where they have painted.

Have each child paint his wax paper bunny with a small amount of the colored oil and then lay some tissue paper shapes on top. Encourage overlapping to change the intensity of the pastel colors. Adhere the tissue paper to the wax paper by having each child paint over the tissue paper with the colored oil. Then hold the completed bunnies over the sink to let any unabsorbed oil drip off the wax paper. When the stained glass bunnies have dried, tape them to a window to let the light shine through them.

This activity lends itself nicely to any season of the year.

In mid-winter, use wax paper heart shapes and red tissue paper. In summer, cut out fish shapes and use blue and green tissue paper.

Jody Brickman
Andover, MA

9" wax paper bunny

1" to 2" tissue paper rectangle

MAY DAY

stapler	flowers
scissors	construction paper

When I was young, I lived in Missouri, and May Day was my favorite spring ritual. My sisters and I would make cone-shaped flower holders out of construction paper, fill them with spring flowers from our yard and leave them hanging on the door knobs of our neighbors' houses. We always left one at Mrs. Dougherty's house because she was old and lived alone. The key to the fun was secrecy. We would hang our trumpet of flowers on the front door, ring the doorbell, and run to hide in the bushes to watch the discovery. Mrs. Dougherty always exclaimed loudly and made a great fuss over her May Day blossoms, much to our

delight. She would pretend to look for us, but was careful not to find us. Instead, she would thank the bushes for making her May Day a special one.

To make a cone-shaped flower holder, twist a 9 by 11 inch piece of construction paper until you have a cone shape. Staple both ends of the cone to hold it together. Cut off the corner to make a Horn of Plenty look. Then cut a strip of paper 11 inches or longer and staple it on to the top of the cone for a handle. Fill with flowers and give to someone special.

Mary Pritchard
Andover, MA

CHILD'S TRAY GARDEN

moss	pebbles
sand	seashells
twigs	cut flowers
ferns	aluminum foil pan
berries	

When my children visit their English grandmother in summer, they traditionally make a tray or dish garden together to enter in the village fete. In England, this is a typical summer activity for children.

Collect flora, pebbles, moss, twigs and anything else that strikes your child's fancy from your garden. Explain to your child that her tray garden will be a miniature garden, where a small twig might represent a tall tree.

Have your child scoop approximately one inch of fine sand into her tray. Water the sand to make it moist. Together, create a miniature garden using her collectibles.

Here are some ideas:

1) Arrange the moss to create open green spaces.

2) Create a garden path using pebbles.

3) Use twigs and ferns to represent trees and bushes.

4) Build a bridge using stones and a piece of bark.

5) Mound sand on one side to create a small hill and cover it with moss.

6) Place cut flower blossoms with a 1 1/2-to 2-inch stem in various spots to provide color or create a flower bed.

7) Cover an inverted metal jar top with foil, fill it with water and place it in the garden to create a small pond.

If you keep the sand moist, your child's tray garden should last for a couple of weeks.

Susan Russell
Andover, MA

SEASHORE DIORAMA

glue	shoe box
sand	driftwood
paint	seashells
rocks	cotton balls
seaweed	

Seashore scenes are well adapted to the shoe box diorama - a three-dimensional scene set against a painted background.

Find a large shoe box and lay it on its side, lengthwise. The bottom of the shoe box has now become the backdrop to your scene. In order to create more light, cut away half of the top side, the ceiling of your

diorama, to open up the setting. Collect objects from the beach to use in your diorama. For a seashore diorama, you might include some of the following ideas:

1) Paint the sky and water on the backdrop, a few seagulls, and maybe a sailboat or two.

2) Paint trees, rocks, or a cottage on the two inside ends of the shoe box.

3) Glue cotton balls in the sky for fluffy white clouds.

4) Cut out a sun from yellow fabric to glue in the sky.

5) Spread glue evenly on the side that has now become the flat foreground of the diorama

and sprinkle a layer of sand to create a beach effect.

6) Glue seashells, dried seaweed, and small bits of driftwood onto the sand.

7) Place Little People in the diorama.

The possibilities are endless.

Mary Pritchard
Andover, MA

CAMP TAKE-A-TURN

This activity started one summer when our children were three years old. Each mom was assigned a week, and for two mornings that week, she hosted camp at her house. Activities were planned for the children. (Ideas from this book would be helpful!) We hired a teenage assistant for the four weeks.

She helped with the activities and watched any siblings who might be home.

This was a great way to have fun with the children and earn some free time for moms as well.

Susan Richardson
Andover, MA

Shelley Selwyn
Andover, MA

Mary Ann Lennon
Andover, MA

Candace Westgate
Andover, MA

To keep satin sashes on holiday dresses from unraveling, dip the ends of the sashes into the melted wax from a white candle. When dry, the wax is clear. This procedure is recommended for girls over three who will not put their sashes in their mouths.

Cheryl Torres
Methuen, MA

Use old Christmas cards (or seasonal cards) for name tags on new presents. Let your children cut out the pictures and mount them on construction paper.

Debbie Drew   Mary Kelly
Andover, MA   Martha's Vineyard, MA

At Christmas time, I succeeded in getting my two-and-a-half-year- old's picture taken by telling him we were going to take a picture of his bear. I got my son into the picture by telling him his bear was afraid and needed my son to sit with him. Then, quick as a flash, we snapped the picture!

Laura Shook
N. Andover, MA

Make your own cards using pressed flowers from your garden. Fold an 8½ by 11 inch piece of heavy weight paper in half. Help your child position a pressed flower on the outside of the card. Cover the flower with contact paper and hold it in place.

Linda Beg
Andover, MA

When the ground is covered with snow, fill empty dish detergent bottles or water pistols with colored water. Dress your children warmly and let them draw in the snow.

Susan Richardson   Cathy Greene
Andover, MA   N. Andover, MA

Life with children puts an end to any notions of an immaculate house. However, it is possible to achieve that picked up look. When buying toys or art materials, be sure they come in their own container for easy clean up. If they don't, purchase an appropriate-sized basket, bucket or tin, to give that toy a home.

Linda Pakravan
Andover, MA

Make April Fool's Day a day of fun by staging a role reversal with your child--you be the child and your child can be the parent. Enjoy the humor of this situation as you watch your child try to be you.

Bev Therkelsen
Andover, MA

Spruce up a spring party table with pansies or Johnny-Jump-Ups planted in paper cups. Place one cup at each place setting. Your children can plant the flower cups before the party, thereby making a significant contribution to the holiday table. And guests may take home their own flower in a cup.

Laura Herhold
Swampscott, MA

One of the secrets to making amazing sand sculptures is to use a metal spatula or trowel to help cut and shape your sculpture. Shoe boxes and cake pans also come in handy for creating more versatile shapes.

Jeremy Foy
N. Andover, MA

At holiday times and birthdays, children often receive many toys as gifts. Put some of the toys away in a closet. Every month or two, exchange some of the toys in the closet with the familiar toys. By recycling groups of toys, children will think they have new toys and moms will have less clutter.

Pam Lundstrom
Andover, MA

TRAVEL TIPS

HOW I SPENT MY VACATION

yarn	large needle
crayons	typing paper
markers	2 sheets heavy paper
hole punch	

Before our family leaves for vacation, I prepare a journal so our child can create his own story about the trip. Preschoolers will need assistance making the journal, but older children can do it on their own.

To begin, place a sheet of heavy paper on the top and bottom of a pile of typing paper. Provide at least two blank pages of typing paper for each day of your trip. Then punch three equidistant holes along the left margin of the book. Next, thread yarn in and out of the punched holes and secure the yarn with a knot. I usually add a small map so my child can measure trip distances.

Your journal is now ready for your child to draw or write in. This journal will be a great remembrance for years to come, so be sure to add your child's age and the dates of the trip.

Pam Lundstrom
Andover, MA

NOT JUST A LUNCH BOX

There are so many uses for those colorful lunch boxes. Of course, they will carry food just about anywhere. We have used them to bring a toddler's dinner with us when Mom and Dad are headed for a restaurant and we know they will have nothing suitable on the menu for kids.

We have also used lunch boxes to carry small activities for long car trips, Mom's haircut appointment, or the wait for dinner at a restaurant.

At times, lunch boxes merely quiet the rebellious toddler who will be more willing to venture out the door with Mom in the morning when carrying his own "briefcase" just like hers.

Lunch boxes can be used as a safe place to store toys too small for the baby - just clip it closed and store it right on the shelf. And there must be hundreds of other uses for these handy boxes . . . .

Deborah Turiano
Andover, MA

CAR LOTTO

When we go for long car trips, I give each of my children a pencil and a piece of paper. The children must write down eight or ten two-figure numbers. When a car passes us, I call out the first two figures on the license plate. If one of my children has that number written down, he ticks it off. The winner is the one who has ticked off all his numbers.

Maryse Lernon
Cambrai, France

POOH DROPS

If you are driving in the rain, your passengers can amuse themselves playing Pooh Drops. Each player chooses a raindrop at the top of his window. The race is on when the drops begin their trek down the car windows. The winner is the player whose raindrop reaches the bottom of the window first.

Evan and Jeffrey Tremaine
Spokane, WA

NAME THAT TUNE

Hum the first line of a song you are sure your child will know. If your child recognizes the song he can start singing it. If not, keep humming the song until he identifies it. Then let your child have a turn humming a song for you to identify.

Jeremy Foy
N. Andover, MA

Linda Blau Traub
Andover, MA

AIRPORT BINGO

| pencil | list of airport items |
| paper | |

An airline representative has just informed you that your flight has been delayed. Now what do you do? Gather your children for a game of Airport Bingo.

Give each player a copy of an identical list of items which may be observed in an airport terminal. When a player spies an item on the list, he checks it off his list. The winner is the first player to check off all the items on his list. You might include some of the following items in your game: an exit sign, a men's room sign, a woman with a briefcase, a man carrying a suitbag, a person pulling a suitcase, a woman in high heels, a sky cap or porter, a baby in a stroller, a person sleeping, a fire extinguisher....

Matthew Dallett
Andover, MA

JET PACKS

Before leaving on a long trip, fill up a "fanny pack" with party favor goodies. Children can open these trinkets on the plane, train, or in the car. Some ideas for fillers include:
- a notepad and pen
- small compass
- miniature books
- stickers
- small tic-tac-toe
- McDonald's Happy Meal prizes
- nuts, bolts and screws
- Little People (at least two so they can "talk")
- coins (I give 50 cents spending money for the airport)

The packs in our house are saved for trips, so opening them is special and takes the edge off travel.

Anna Duke Reach
Marietta, GA

BIRD, TREE, AND FLOWER GAME

This is a car game from my childhood that helped pass the time over the long stretches of Kansas prairie.

To begin, someone picks a letter of the alphabet. All of the players must then think of a bird, tree, and flower beginning with that letter. For example, if the letter is "B," my bird might be a bluejay, my flower a buttercup, and my tree a birch. The youngest child usually goes first to grab some of the easier choices. Every player gets a turn and can not use any of the choices already identified.

Once the children in our family dropped out, it was fun to watch my parents duel to the inevitable point when my mother won with some incredibly obscure flora.

This game can be adapted for younger children by choosing "animal" or "book titles" for a category instead of "trees." I credit my identification skills (we always had bird, tree, and flower books in the car) to this game, and I am looking forward to making it a part of my family's history, too.

Mary Pritchard
Andover, MA

SNAP, CRACKLE, POP

We learned this car game when we first moved to North Carolina. The official way to play the game is to look for dogs, horses, and tractors as you are driving. The first person to see a dog and say "SNAP" gets one point. The first person to see a horse and say "CRACKLE" gets three points. The first person to see a tractor and say "POP" gets five points. The winner is the first person to score 50 or 100 points.

As we have gotten better at the game, we have expanded it to include penalties for making the wrong sound when you see something. For example, if you see a tractor but say "CRACKLE" you lose five points. Listed below are additional things we have added to our list, including what you have to say when you see them, and the number of points you get if you are the first person to make the correct sound:

- motorcycle, "ZOOM," 2 points
- boat, "BUBBA, BUBBA, BUBBA," 3 points
- police car, "RRR, RRR," 10 points
- school bus, "BUFFALO," 2 points

Cathy Eaton
Michael, Colin and Devon Murphy
Asheville, NC

AUTOMOBILE ALPHABET

The object of this game is to be the first person to find all the letters of the alphabet on signs along the road. Two people can play this game or you can play in teams. Each player reads signs on her side of the road. Starting with the letter "A," look for a word that begins with "A," such as "AMES." You may only use the first letter in a word. The exception is the letter "X," which may be anywhere within a word, as in "EXIT." Continue looking for words that begin with the letter you need. The first person or team to reach "Z" wins.

Lisa Williams
Andover, MA

Kathleen Burke
Methuen, MA

LETTER TALK

Have someone in the car pick a letter. Then look out the window and call out as many things as you can see that begin with that letter. For example, if the letter is "B" you might see: bicycles, bats, birds, bees, balloons, bumps, bridges, bricks, barns and books. Keep track of the number of things you saw that began with the letter "B." Then try the game with another letter. Children who are just learning letter sounds may need some helpful hints to play the game.

Anne Singleton
Wellesley, MA

THE PARSON'S CAT

As a boy in England, I was required to treat the parson of our village church with great respect. This game allowed us to poke fun at him — although indirectly - while keeping us occupied in the car as well.

The object of the game is to describe the parson's cat in as many ways as possible, the sillier the better. Each player in turn completes the following sentence, "The parson's cat is a _____ cat."

To begin, each player inserts an adjective beginning with the letter "A." For example, the first player might say, "The Parson's cat is an <u>angry</u> cat," or "The Parson's cat is an <u>awful</u> cat." When no one can think of another adjective beginning with the letter "A," move onto adjectives beginning with the letter "B," and so on. If you have the time and interest, you can work your way through the entire alphabet.

Matthew Dallett
Andover, MA

ANIMAL COUNTING

The object of this game is to count as many animals as you can as you drive along the road.

Two people can play this game looking out opposite sides of the car, or you can play in teams. Each player counts the number of animals she sees on her side of the road. If a church is passed, the player on that side of the car gets to double her number of animals because they got married. However, if a cemetery is passed, the player on that side of the car must bury her animals and start over. The first player to reach a predetermined number (we use 100) wins the game.

Lisa Williams
Andover, MA

I SPY

Take turns thinking of something in the car. Then give the other players some clues by saying "I spy with my little eye, something that is_____ ." Fill in the blank with a descriptive adjective, such as "red" or "shiny." The first person to guess the right answer is the winner.

Joan Elias
Andover, MA

YOUR NEW CAR

If you have a fussy crew in your car, divert their attention with a game of "Your New Car." Pretend that your car has just broken down and that you are going to shop for a new car. Pick a number between 1 and 20 and begin counting the cars traveling past you in the opposite direction. If you chose the number 15, your new car will be the fifteenth car to pass you. Will it be a luxury car or a lemon? Each person in the car may shop for her own new car.

Gerry Pouliot
Andover, MA

THE GUESSING GAME

My daughter, Sarah, invented this game during a long car trip to upstate New York. It's a fun game to play with children of all ages.

One player thinks of an animal and then gives the other players a clue. The other players take turns trying to guess the animal's identity. Additional clues may be given as needed. For example, clues for a younger child may be as simple as: "Something with hooves." The child then gets to name all the animals she knows with hooves until she gets the right answer. Then it's your child's turn to think of an animal and give you clues.

For an older child, you can make the clues more sophisticated. For example: "Something that lives in the treetops in the rain forests," or "A species threatened by extinction."

Elizabeth Fletcher Foy
N. Andover, MA

PAPER DOLL CHAINS

To turn long waiting periods at doctors' offices and auto body shops into a more creative and pleasant use of time, pack along a pair of scissors, some paper, and a few crayons to make paper dolls.

Fold a piece of paper into a fan. Then cut out a chain of paper dolls for your child to color. (Remember not to cut off the folds at the arms and legs.) Your child may want to create a face, outfit, and personality for each cutout, or she may need your help in developing a theme for each doll. For example, suggest dressing them in different outfits for each season of the year and then drawing different facial expressions on each of them. Don't forget to bring the dolls home for extended play!

Sandy Kingsland
Scituate, MA

MY GRANDMOTHER'S CHEST

This can be an hilarious memory game to play in the car. The first person starts the game by saying, "I looked in my grandmother's chest and found _____." She must then name a real or fantastical object, such as a brush, a purple cat, or a flying saucer. The next person repeats the phrase "I looked in my grandmother's chest and found _____." She must name the object the first person found and then add her own object. Play continues with each player repeating all of the objects that have been previously named and then adding one object of her own choosing. The game ends when no one can remember the correct sequence.

Andrea Margida
Apex, NC

To liven up a car trip, bring along a few blank tapes with a hand-held recorder. Children love hearing their own voices and creating their own tapes!

Anna Duke Reach
Marietta, GA

Colorforms can be fun and useful without their board. On car trips, colorforms are perfect for children to stick on the side windows. Children will enjoy creating scenes with their "stickers," telling stories about the scenes, and peeling them off the window.

Christine Davis
Andover, MA

If you are going on a long car trip make sure you have a good collection of story and song tapes. Although we often listen to storytelling together so we can talk about the stories, we also bring along a cassette player with earphones for each of our children. We pop a story or song tape into their cassette players, give them a pillow to lean against and then we all get to have some much needed quiet time.

Cathy Eaton
Asheville, NC

Visiting friends or relatives your child hasn't seen in a while? Make a small, inexpensive photo album with pictures of the people you will be visiting. En route, talk with your child about the people you will be visiting and identify them in the pictures.

Sharon Thies
Andover, MA

Whenever we go on long trips, I pack various types of tape and a box of Band-Aids for each child. Their sudden appearance has stopped many a complaint in mid-sentence.

Elizabeth Fletcher Foy
N. Andover, MA

For those times when I have forgotten my child's bib, I pull out two wooden clothespins I keep handy in my diaper bag. I use the clothespins to make quick, disposable bibs out of restaurant napkins. I also carry a garlic press which can double as a portable food mill.

Jane Cairns
Andover, MA

To give an infant something interesting to look at on car trips, attach a colorful scrap of cloth on the back seat or pin up simple black and white designs or geometric shapes or faces. These visuals may prompt some of your baby's first smiles.

Cheryl Torres   Becky Kangos
Methuen, MA   N. Andover, MA

The next time you are in a restaurant with an infant in a carrier or car seat, turn the wooden high chair upside down and place the infant seat securely inside its legs. Then store your coats and diaper bag on the high chair beneath the car seat. Your infant will love being up high with everyone else, you won't have to keep bending over to tend to the baby, and the carrier won't take up valuable table space.

Wendy Venti
N. Andover, MA

Don't leave crayons in the car, because when the car heats up, the crayons may melt!

Francine Fritsch Gikow
Andover, MA

We purchased two small, inexpensive suitcases and gave one to each of our sons. They decorated their suitcases with stickers and now have their own personalized "going to Grandma's" suitcase.

Lynn Lynch
Reading, MA

When all else fails and disgruntled kids are screaming at the top of their lungs "Are we there yet?" - COUNT. Count how long it takes to reach a bridge you see in the distance, or how long it takes for the light to turn green, or how long it takes for Mom to start smiling again!

Elizabeth Fletcher Foy
N. Andover, MA

INDEX

INDEX

ART CREDITS

<u>Jennifer Cullen-Struhl</u>: pp. i, v, 3, 6, 12, 25, 29, 32, 33, 36, 55, 58, 61, 64, 78, 81, 83, 84, 85, 86, 90, 93, 102, 113, 126, 129, 137, 147, 159, 168, 169, 180, 183, 184, 186, 188, 189, 190, 201, 203, 209, 214, 231.

<u>Joani Ellis</u>: pp. ix, 7, 15, 39, 42, 43, 57, 60, 65, 66, 91, 100, 105, 106, 112, 114, 127, 130, 131, 133, 151, 157, 170, 179, 182, 191, 194, 195, 210, 211, 216, 218.

<u>Alice Blaine Jaffe</u>: pp. iii, 5, 10, 11, 15, 16, 17, 19, 28, 30, 31, 34, 35, 38, 41, 44, 46, 48, 62, 63, 67, 69, 76, 79, 80, 88, 89, 99, 101, 103, 104, 108, 110, 117, 125, 128, 131, 135, 136, 138, 139, 145, 154, 156, 162, 166, 171, 177, 181, 192, 193, 198, 200, 202, 212, 217, 219, 230.

<u>Marcia Strykowski</u>: pp. 4, 8, 9, 13, 14, 26, 27, 47, 49, 56, 59, 77, 87, 92, 107, 109, 116, 134, 149, 160, 161, 163, 164, 165, 178, 185, 187, 197, 215, 220.

<u>Bev Therkelsen</u>: pp. 18, 37, 40, 45, 68, 75, 82, 111, 123, 124, 132, 152, 153, 157, 158, 167, 199, 213.

<u>Title Page and Chapter Divider Pages</u> by Jennifer Cullen-Struhl, Sharon Chew, and Alice Blaine Jaffe.

SOURCES

P 197. "Lady Spring-Ring Game," by Diana Carey and Judy Large. From *Festivals, Family and Food.* Hawthorn Press, 1982, Copyright © by Diana Carey and Judy Large. Reprinted by permission.